"This book is a needed plea to the church to rediscover the real gospel as rooted in participation in and engagement with Christ. It leads to a better understanding of the call of our faith to be active and focused on things that matter. The gospel has been hijacked for many other things that have little or nothing to do with what God asks of all people. We are made in his image and designed for relationship and participation with him. This book sets all of that right, leading us not only to reflect who we are designed to be but to live actively in the very way God asks us to travel, aware that he is very much with us and in us as we go."

—Darrell L. Bock, Dallas Theological Seminary

"Many struggle to find the coherence in what seems like a big jumble of ideas in the Bible: grace, obedience, works, salvation, ethics, baptism, and so on. Snodgrass has put his finger on the missing piece that holds these all together—participation. Christianity's God-centered gospel is focused on personal transformation because the means to salvation and its goal are found in participation, union with Christ through the Spirit. This view changes everything, so I strongly commend this book."

—Ben C. Blackwell, Houston Theological Seminary

"Delaying gratification works well when you're on a diet or saving for retirement but not so well when it comes to defining the content of the gospel, which concerns not only an *afterlife* but eternal life *now*. To have eternal life is to participate in the family of God—in the Son, through the Spirit—with other adoptees. Snodgrass rightly asks evangelicals—'gospel people'—to recover the New Testament understanding of faith, which is considerably more rich, dramatic, and self-involving than merely signing on the doctrinal dotted line."

—Kevin J. Vanhoozer, Trinity Evangelical Divinity School

"In this important and readable book, Snodgrass unpacks what is, for many Christians, a significantly underappreciated scriptural theme: God's participation with us and our participation in the life of God. The robust gospel of transformative participation recovered and expounded in these pages is a needed corrective to the simplistic gospel on offer in too many quarters of the church. A must-read for pastors and lay people as well as professors and scholars."

—**Michael J. Gorman**, St. Mary's Seminary & University; author of *Participating in Christ*

YOU
NEED
A
BETTER
Gospel

YOU
NEED
A
BETTER
Gospel

RECLAIMING THE GOOD NEWS OF
PARTICIPATION WITH CHRIST

KLYNE R. SNODGRASS

B
Baker Academic
a division of Baker Publishing Group
Grand Rapids, Michigan

Published by Baker Academic
a division of Baker Publishing Group
PO Box 6287, Grand Rapids, MI 49516-6287
www.bakeracademic.com

Library of Congress Cataloging-in-Publication Data
Names: Snodgrass, Klyne, author.
Title: You need a better gospel : reclaiming the Good News of participation with Christ / Klyne R. Snodgrass.
Description: Grand Rapids, Michigan : Baker Academic, a division of Baker Publishing Group, [2022] | Includes bibliographical references and index.
Identifiers: LCCN 2021020403 | ISBN 9781540965042 (paperback) | ISBN 9781540965356 (casebound) | ISBN 9781493435043 (ebook)
Subjects: LCSH: Salvation—Christianity. | Faith—Biblical teaching. | Engagement (Philosophy)—Miscellanea.
Classification: LCC BT751.3 .S663 2022 | DDC 234—dc23
LC record available at https://lccn.loc.gov/2021020403

Unless otherwise indicated, Scripture translations are the author's own.

Scripture quotations labeled NIV are from THE HOLY BIBLE, NEW INTERNATIONAL VERSION®, NIV® Copyright © 1973, 1978, 1984, 2011 by Biblica, Inc.® Used by permission. All rights reserved worldwide.

Scripture quotations labeled NRSV are from the New Revised Standard Version of the Bible, copyright © 1989 National Council of the Churches of Christ in the United States of America. Used by permission. All rights reserved.

Baker Publishing Group publications use paper produced from sustainable forestry practices and post-consumer waste whenever possible.

22   23   24   25   26   27   28   7   6   5   4   3   2   1

In honor of scholars who have gone before and taught all of us so much both in print and in person, especially Richard N. Longenecker and Walter L. Liefeld

CONTENTS

PREFACE

Our world seems trapped in conflict, division, violence, and disorder. Is there any good news for such a world? We need—you and I need—good news that enables life. The Christian gospel is indeed good news and offers peace, hope, and a foundation on which to live constructively. But the gospel is good news only if it actually effects change in the lives of those who say they believe it. What is the gospel? I want to come down emphatically on the side of those who insist the gospel is a gospel of participation. The gospel is not merely about a declaration or a transaction that satisfies God and secures the future. It is about God drawing us into a relation that is nothing short of participation with God and God's purposes now, and this astounding assertion gives life value, direction, and hope.

At times I will offer a broad view of the topic under discussion, and at other times I will focus more closely on specific biblical texts, especially in chapters eight and nine. Both approaches are needed for an adequate view of participation.

The translations of biblical passages are my own unless otherwise specified. Also, italics in quotations of Scripture are my own and have been added for emphasis. I want to thank some wonderful people who read all or part of the manuscript, especially

Stephen Chester, Markus Nikkanen, Lars Stromberg, Bob Hubbard, Jim Bruckner, and my wife, Phyllis. I also want to thank the people at Baker Academic, especially James Korsmo, for their help in bringing the text to its final form.

Pentecost 2021

Introduction

Christianity (that is, the Christianity of the New Testament . . .)
does not exist. . . . Christianity [in Denmark] is enjoyment of life,
tranquilized . . . by the assurance that the thing about eternity is set-
tled. . . . I will not take part in what is known as official Christianity.

Søren Kierkegaard[1]

Nothing compares to riding a horse. I have been riding horses since I was ten, and I can assure you that thinking about riding or talking about riding, which even nonriders can do, is not the same as riding a horse. The same is true with faith. Thinking about faith and talking about faith may be enjoyable and stimulating, but they are nowhere close to living a faith, which is what Christianity is about.

Søren Kierkegaard's words above, addressed to nineteenth-century Danish Christians, are unsettling, even harsh, but they point to the cleavage between the New Testament message and modern perceptions of Christianity. The problem of such failure in our day is worse.

For several years I taught a course on the Christian gospel for graduating seminarians, soon to be pastors. It was intended to

1. Søren Kierkegaard, *Kierkegaard's Attack upon "Christendom," 1854–1855,* trans. Walter Lowrie (Princeton: Princeton University Press, 1946), 29, 35, 39.

1

help them synthesize their studies and leave school with a clear understanding of the gospel that would be the focus of their ministries and their efforts to lead people to Jesus Christ and make them followers of Christ. But the problems those students will face are enormous for two reasons: our society has little interest in a gospel, and the church has failed miserably to do justice to its own message.

Naming the Problems

Religious issues are not a major concern—or a concern at all—for most of society. People do not seek God in their lives, do not worry about going to heaven, and claim not to seek the meaning of life, and an increasing number, about 23 percent, classify themselves as "nones," as not having a religion.[2] The hunger and need are still there, even if not acknowledged, and anxiety and depression have become major factors in our society. No wonder! For some, religion is personally customized—"What I want to believe." Many claim to be spiritual but not religious, which renders the word "spiritual" vague and virtually meaningless,[3] but in any case there is little sense of a revealed message from God that makes a demand on our lives. God is just not that important, especially if people have enough money and entertainment. To them the gospel is old hat, irrelevant, and they have other things to do.

The church seems to have lost its voice and any ground from which to challenge such thinking. It has failed to understand and take seriously its own gospel and, worse, has often denied its gospel by its actions. Christian lives are often no different from

2. See "Trends: Religion & Spirituality," GSS Data Explorer, accessed July 10, 2021, https://gssdataexplorer.norc.org/trends/Religion%20&%20Spirituality?measure= relig_rec.

3. The word "spiritual" has a Christian origin and concerns someone or something (such as a song) impacted by the Holy Spirit. If you are not a Christian, to what spirit are you referring? In modern usage the term is used broadly of a subjective, deep, and meaningful experience.

those of non-Christians. In the name of Christianity people have practiced racism and injustice and have thrown off all guidelines for Christian ethics. Those who are supposed to be models of the faith are too often abject failures at Christian living. We are weary of hearing about failed leaders. So much done in the name of Christ is an embarrassment to Christ. As Ernst Käsemann put it, the biggest obstacle to the mission of the church is the church,[4] but the church will never be what it is supposed to be without a recovery of its own gospel. We do indeed need a better gospel.

I confess frustration with the church; I have been frustrated with the church all of my adult life. Often I have found myself bored to death in church or feeling the need to flee from the church, having grown weary of the machinations, of going through the motions, of putting on the show, of wondering why we are here, and of not doing justice to life with God. But there is nowhere to go. Life with God is not to be found apart from his Word, his work, and his people. If only they would wake up and stand up.

Many *claim* the Christian faith but do not come close to living as disciples of Christ. According to a recent report, 64 percent of millennials self-identify as Christians, but only 22 percent actually practice their faith—with this practice defined *minimally* as attending church every month and *saying* faith is important in their lives. Additionally, nearly two-thirds of people eighteen to twenty-nine years old in the US who grew up in church and were active as a child or teen have withdrawn from church involvement as an adult.[5] The church has become increasingly irrelevant.

We have offered a deficient, inept, and inert gospel that in the end is not even a gospel, not good news. The church offers merely

4. Ernst Käsemann, "Some Thoughts on the Theme 'The Doctrine of Reconciliation in the New Testament,'" in *The Future of Our Religious Past*, ed. James M. Robinson (New York: Harper & Row, 1964), 49–64, here 60.

5. See "A Snapshot of Faith Practice across Age Groups," Barna Group, July 23, 2019, https://www.barna.com/research/faithview-on-faith-practice/; and "Year in Review: Barna's Top 10 Releases of 2019," Barna Group, December 18, 2019, https://www.barna.com/research/top-10-releases-of-2019/.

an anemic voice in the wind. What is said is neither compelling nor taken seriously. It is not attractive, and it hardly changes anything. The church has failed to address crucial issues like racism, poverty, arrogance, sexual misconduct—and sin. We hardly even mention sin. This is not to say all churches fail or that the church does not teach and do good things, but it surely does not do justice to its gospel.

What would it take to get pastors, church workers, theological students, and any other interested people to reconsider what they understand and present as the gospel? What would it take actually to produce disciples, people taught by and characterized by Christ?

If Christians have not understood their gospel well or lived it much, is it any surprise that non-Christians have not understood or have disparaged the faith? Society has lost respect for the church because the church's gospel has been minimalized, muted, distorted, and not practiced. The church of the simplified gospel has collapsed, and the only question is why it took so long.

Over the centuries, people have been told variously to genuflect before some icon, to purchase indulgences, to give money, or to make a decision, with the understanding that they could do it and then get on with their lives. Christianity does not offer an option of doing something and then getting on with your life. We have been handed a gospel of no responsibility, but Jesus's teaching never offered anything without responsibility. When the church has reacted against such errors, it has always become stronger.

It is time, especially given the distressing state of our society, for Christians to react, stand up, and take their faith seriously, actually to be changed by faith rather than merely use faith as a pretense.

But people often have no idea what the gospel really is. If the gospel is as overwhelmingly engaging, as overwhelmingly important as I think, if I am right in explaining the New Testament, then the gospel is the most important and most demanding reality of human existence.

What is the problem the gospel is intended to solve? It is intended to take you past yourself, your lack of purpose, your foolishness, and your destructive acts and to give you life, a life worth living, something beyond the trivia, the self-centeredness, and the *loss of life* in entertainment and mere pleasure seeking. The gospel is intended to redirect you, to give you life even in the midst of suffering and death, to give you hope beyond death, and to hold out a vision of how wonderful life is and can be. It is intended to enable you to be *truly* human, a person empowered to be your real self, the kind of human God created you to be. This life worth everything is life engaged with and *participating* in the life and purposes of God, actually doing something productive and worthwhile. The gospel is intended to restore right relations with God and with other people for meaningful and productive living.

My course on the gospel for graduating seminarians addressed six questions:

1. Why does anyone need the gospel?
2. What is the gospel?
3. What, specifically, do the death and resurrection of Jesus have to do with the gospel?
4. To what degree is the gospel eschatological (that is, about the end times)?
5. How is the gospel appropriated?
6. How should the gospel be articulated?

I will not address all these explicitly, but with the fifth an explanation is needed. The question is really, Just how does the gospel work so that it is effective in one's life? How is the death of a Jew two thousand years ago of any benefit to us, and how does it have an impact on us? How is the benefit made ours?

The Good News

I do need to offer a short explanation of the gospel, even though the whole book will be explaining this. If we have to give a short explanation of the gospel, what would it be? My answer is this:

> God is *for* us and loves us, and God intends to have a people, a "family." Even when people ignore God, go their own way, and do what is wrong, God will still have a people. God grieves over the world, filled as it is with suffering, sin, and evil. That God is for us is demonstrated—revealed—powerfully through Jesus, the promised Deliverer. In Jesus, God identified with human suffering and evil, confronted sin, demonstrated how humans should live, in his own being took on our sin and dealt with it, and gave his life for us, demonstrating just how much God is for us. God is the God who creates life in the midst of death. Jesus's resurrection *is* the good news. With Jesus's death and resurrection God has defeated both death and evil, offers forgiveness, and engages us with meaningful action. God gives his transforming, life-creating Spirit to us to give life and purpose now, to create a community of Spirit-endowed people who reflect God's character and purposes in the world, and to give hope of ongoing life with God in a new earth and a new heaven. In a real sense the gospel calls us into being and into life engaged with God. This is a *gospel of participation* and power, good news indeed.

Or, if you prefer a shorter version, God is for you, even if you are a worthless, amoral twit, and through Jesus he invites you to live with him to become who you should be.

The gospel is about God's participation with us and our participation with God. The gospel offers and enables life with God, being "family" in community with God, and participation with God in the way you live. You are not a Christian because you said the sinner's prayer, go to *x* church, hang out with people called Christians, or do "spiritual" things. You are a Christian only if you have a Christian identity, if you give up your life to take Christ's and actually take on the responsibility of following

Christ. The gospel is a gospel of free grace but not a gospel of no responsibility. It is a gospel of participation with Christ because of being joined to Christ.

Most Christians have heard about union with Christ, but it is not a frequently discussed subject, is not well understood, and sounds like an optional add-on for the spiritual. There is, however, a renewed and heavy emphasis on participation among scholars, and Christians must not ignore what scholars take for granted. Nor should the church have to wait twenty years for the good parts of the gospel to trickle down. Even if you do not use the language of participation, you have to incorporate the ideas.

Some might say "participation" is not the right word. "Attachment" is easier to grasp, and I am all for attachment to Christ, but "attachment" does not insist on engagement. The same is true for "solidarity." Attachment and solidarity are useful descriptions, but in the end, participation is much more engaging and profound. I use "participation" in the broadest sense so that it includes union, communion, attachment, and identification. It is about being *bound to God*. The word "religion" derives from the Latin word *religare*, which means "to bind." We all bind ourselves to someone or something, and various forms of reverence and obligation naturally follow. Being bound to or grounding our identity in anything or anyone other than the God revealed in Christ is idolatry—sin—and idols demand sacrifices. They are burdens and destroy life. "Participation" is the word that best does justice to being bound to God.

No term is perfect, and any word may already have been misused or depreciated. As we will see, however, "participation" is biblical, has a long history in the church, and is everyday language, since we use it for all kinds of other things. Recently "participation" was used to describe marketing: "In the participation age, our job as marketers is to build engagement that compels action, inspires loyalty, and delivers powerful outcomes."[6] That is

---

6. Bryan Specht, "The 3 Cs of Participation Marketing," *Adweek*, November 13, 2019, https://www.adweek.com/sponsored/the-three-cs-of-participation-marketing/.

precisely what an emphasis on the gospel of participation offers: engagement with Christ "that compels action, inspires loyalty, and delivers powerful outcomes." *Christian faith is about participation with God.* As mind-bending as that sounds, that is the Christian gospel. The privilege of such participation is all from God's grace and is all encompassing, all motivating, and all engaging.

Of course, you participate with all kinds of things already. To be alive is to participate. You are attaching yourself to all kinds of things and participating in all kinds of things. Are they worth it?

In the following pages I will show just how pervasively the gospel is a gospel of participation and will spell out the significance of such an understanding. I assert from the get-go: the gospel offers participation in the very life of God.

one

Participation in Christ

Nothing is more harmful than when one mistakes and deceives oneself that one believes and understands the gospel well.

Martin Luther[1]

Martin Luther's warning is a caution for all of us. Modern Christians have not come close to understanding the gospel well. For many people the gospel has been truncated into an insignificant add-on and is not grasped as the life-shattering, life-transforming, life-re-creating reality it is. How easy it is to pervert the gospel into something we like or can control! The gospel has been simplified into an irrelevant message about saying the right words so you can go to heaven, even though *the Bible has relatively little focus on going to heaven.*

If the gospel message is "God just wants you to be happy," then the gospel has failed the huge portion of humanity who suffer immensely. If the message is about prosperity, if it is the "health and wealth gospel," again the gospel has failed most of this troubled world. But the health and wealth gospel is a fraudulent gospel trading on not half-truths but minimal truths. That Christians can

1. *Tischreden* [*Table Talk*] 6680, in Weimarer Ausgabe 2/6:114.

be so unthinking in this and other ways is a huge embarrassment.
Christians should be the most thoughtful and discerning of all.
No scholar or serious Christian sounds like the media preachers
and teachers. They know better. They know the gospel is much
deeper and much more engaging.

Does the church have a word for this troubled world? Granted,
the church is itself often troubled, neither living up to its message
nor even explaining its message well. We all know that in the
church, self-centeredness can be just as dominant, marriages can
fail just as much, and people can bend justice to serve their own
needs just as much. If the church is not going to be different, why
should anyone bother?

It does not take a genius to know that the church has this wonderful message from and about Jesus but fails to live up to it.
Especially in our day, even the word "evangelical," a word that
focuses on a commitment to the gospel, has been distorted beyond
all recognition, not least in support of political agendas. People
claim the word "evangelical" but have no sense of what it really
means, which is a tragedy. Neither of our major political parties
deserves a great deal of respect, but why did many evangelicals—
so-called at least—rush to support someone who with words and
actions violated nearly everything they say they stand for and, in
the process, desecrate the name of Jesus?

We have a problem. The Christian gospel has been highjacked,
subverted, and rendered simplistic for all kinds of self-serving purposes. What is offered in many churches is an embarrassment. If
we do not recover the real gospel, we are in danger of rendering the
church absolutely irrelevant, a process that is already underway.

However, I am not attacking the church, for in spite of its foi-
bles, with the church there is always a chance, always a hope, for
something different. I am calling the church to take back its own
gospel and to do justice to its own message. If Paul's Letters, such
as Galatians, mightily resist any perversion of the gospel, should
we do less?

In many churches the customary language for becoming a Christian is "to ask Jesus into your heart," but where did we get this language? It does not occur in the New Testament, and the one text that sounds like it (Rev. 3:20) is actually addressed to *Christians*.[2] This language is not entirely wrong, even if it is not explicitly very biblical, and if people really understand the significance, it can be useful. On the other hand, it has been so trivialized and truncated that it borders on being useless. For years I have been telling Christians to stop telling people to invite Jesus into their hearts. It is marginally biblical, and it is not working.

The emphasis on making a decision so one can go to heaven assumes the gospel is more about going to heaven in a security blanket than about life with God now. This has led to gross distortions of the gospel. God is moved to the margins of life, since the "big issue" is settled, and we can pretty much go on as before. But the nagging question "Did we do enough?" and the lack of anything truly significant lead to the heavy emphasis on eternal security in some traditions. "Once saved, always saved" is supposed to be a comfort, but it is more an attempt to prop up a weak view of the gospel. I have no doubt about God's being faithful in saving, but there can be no comfort in believing an illegitimate gospel that does not produce transformation in one's life. Decisions are important, but response to the gospel is more than a decision. It is a life. Conversion is an *ongoing process of life with God*, as the New Testament emphasizes repeatedly. Proclamation of the gospel has often neglected this and has been too abstract, too simplistic, too individualistic, and just wrong.

The root of the problem is the erroneous, anemic, and weak-kneed understandings people have of the word "faith." "Faith" is viewed as a mental activity, and a passive and inactive one at that—"Just believe; you do not have to do anything." Faith is not

2. Rev. 3:20—"I stand at the door and knock. If anyone hears my voice and opens the door, I will come in and eat with that person, and that person with me"—is addressed to the church of Laodicea.

mental activity; it is life activity. It is not about checking a box for
a ticket to heaven. How did anyone ever conclude from the New
Testament that you do not have to do anything?

What will place us back on track? We need better, more helpful, and more powerful language—specifically the language of
participation with, solidary with, and attachment to Christ. I
want to argue for a gospel of participation, a gospel that leads to
an involvement with Christ that does not allow passivity and that
makes sense of Christ's death and resurrection and their importance for us. "Participation" is the language the church should be
using when it speaks of the gospel, for the biblical message, especially in the New Testament, is about a relation with Christ that
binds us to him, *involves* us with him and his purposes, *engages*
us in his work, and *delivers* wonderful outcomes.

Do people really want that? Each person will have to answer for
himself or herself, but that is what Christianity is about. *Faith is
participation with Christ, not merely thinking about him.* Having
an opinion about Christ or holding some doctrine about Christ
is not faith in Christ. Believing certain ideas does not make you a
Christian. Being joined to Christ and taking on his character does.

What Faith Really Means

Even a glance at the facts of the Bible jolts one away from imagin-
ing the word "faith" is merely about mental activity. In both the
Old and New Testaments believing is *not* thinking about or as-
senting to certain ideas. For a long time I have been saying "Faith
is not what you think," which intentionally has a double meaning.
Faith is not what most people think it is, and it is not merely what
you do with your brain. It is what you do with your life.

I will treat "faith" in the Old Testament later, but with regard
to the New Testament language for "faith/belief" the Greek word
usually translated by "faith" is *pistis*, and the verb form, which
English usually translates with "believe," is *pisteuein*. The range

of meanings for this word group is extremely broad. Anthony
Thiselton, a leading New Testament scholar, identifies thirteen
different nuances for *pistis*, but even that does not do justice to
the breadth of the word.[3] *Pistis* can sometimes be used for belief
in the facts of a matter, but usually it points to much more. It
was not particularly a religious word in the Hellenistic Greek
world and most often had to do with *relations* in business and
political contexts. It is most of all a *relational word having to do
with trust* and pledges of trust and is not about what we do with
our minds. It is about how one *acts* in a relation. Consequently,
it often carries connotations of faithfulness, loyalty, fidelity, allegiance, reliability, trustworthiness, commitment, confidence,
proof, and pledge.

For example, in the NRSV translation of Titus 2:10, slaves are
asked "to show complete and perfect fidelity [*pistis*]." In 1 Maccabees 10:27 *pistis* refers to keeping faith with someone: "Now
continue still to keep faith with us."[4] This is not about thinking;
it is about staying faithful in a relation. Such examples could be
multiplied easily. The first-century Jewish philosopher Philo calls
pistis the most perfect of the virtues.[5] A virtue is not something
you think, but something you live. Faith has a durative quality; it
is a way of being over time. That may not be what many people
expect or want, but it is a fact. Not surprisingly, then, and for
good reason, some scholars urge translating New Testament occurrences of *pistis* with "loyalty" or "allegiance."[6]

3. Anthony C. Thiselton, *Doubt, Faith, and Certainty* (Grand Rapids: Eerdmans,
2017), 10–11. His discussion on pp. 61–65 gives more focus to ideas of faithfulness
and trust.

4. *Emmeinate eti tou syntērēsai pros hēmas pistin.*

5. Philo, *Who Is the Heir?* 91; see Philo, *On the Life of Abraham* 270, where *pistis*
is called the queen of the virtues.

6. Regarding "loyalty," see, e.g., Nijay K. Gupta, *Paul and the Language of Faith*
(Grand Rapids: Eerdmans, 2020), esp. 68–70, 78–83, 91–92, 178; and Douglas Oakes,
"*Pistis* as Relational Way of Life in Galatians," *Journal for the Study of the New
Testament* 40, no. 3 (2018): 255–75. Regarding "allegiance," see Matthew W. Bates,
*Salvation by Allegiance Alone: Rethinking Faith, Works, and the Gospel of Jesus the
King* (Grand Rapids: Baker Academic, 2017).

I am not suggesting that thinking is unimportant; it is crucial. No one enters a relation of trust without being convinced of a basis for trust, but faith goes way beyond thinking. Scholars and others have for centuries been emphasizing that faith is a relational term,[7] but the truth has been evaded. Now, happily, numerous studies are bringing attention to the multifaceted and relational nature of faith.[8] An obvious question arises: can one have faith without faithfulness? No way! The word is as much about faithfulness as it is about faith, with context determining the nuance. You cannot say you have faith in Christ if you are not determined by relation to him, if you are not faithful to him. Much of this, of course, fits with the idea of covenant in both Testaments. "Faith" is a covenant word.

If faith language often has to do with faithfulness, we—and Bible translations especially—need to be more reflective about what is intended in texts using *pistis*, texts about faith. People glide over the word "faith" in English translations, even when it appears odd, but they need to ask if the focus is really more on faithfulness. As one example, in Ephesians 3:12 the NRSV reads, "in whom [Christ] we have access to God in boldness and confidence through faith in him."[9] A more straightforward translation would be "in whom we have boldness and access with confidence through his faithfulness" (*pisteōs autou*, literally "faith/faithfulness of him"). The Greek phrase in parentheses could mean "faith in him," but would Paul say our boldness and access to God are through our faith, or Christ's faithfulness? Surely it is through Christ's faithfulness.

---

7. Relations are the focus, esp. during and after the Reformation. See pp. 29–31.

8. To mention only three, see Teresa Morgan, *Roman Faith and Christian Faith: Pistis and Fides in the Early Roman Empire and Early Churches* (Oxford: Oxford University Press, 2015); Jeanette Hagen Pifer, *Faith as Participation: An Exegetical Study of Some Key Pauline Texts*, Wissenschaftliche Untersuchungen zum Neuen Testament 2/486 (Tübingen: Mohr Siebeck, 2019); and Gupta, *Paul and the Language of Faith*.

9. The NIV is no better: "In him and through faith in him we may approach God with freedom and confidence."

Numerous texts with the word *pistis* require us to slow down and think about what is intended. For example, the phrase *pistis Christou* in Galatians 2:16 and other texts,[10] if translated literally, could be either "the faith of Christ" or "the faithfulness of Christ," and this phrase has been a cause for heated debate among scholars. Some argue it means "faith in Christ," which is legitimate, and others argue it means "the faithfulness of Christ" and refers to his obedience on the cross or to his faithfulness as resurrected Lord.[11] Most of the texts in question have both the noun, *pistis*, and the verb, *pisteuein*, the latter referring to human faith. Many people are not even aware of the debate, for most English translations just assume "faith in Christ" and use "faith" for the noun and "believe" for the verb, which hides the redundancy if both refer to human faith. I favor the "faithfulness of Christ" option, but in the end, the debate needs reshaping. Faith presupposes the conviction that someone or something is faithful, meriting trust in the relation. Both faith and faithfulness are needed. Some scholars now argue convincingly that *pistis* refers to the complex and reciprocal relation of trust in which Christ binds God and humanity together, is faithful to both God and humanity as he does this binding, and people bind themselves to Christ by their faith.[12]

Most important for the life of the church is that we realize the depth and the profound focus on *relations and practices* that the word *pistis* carries. We need to change how we talk about faith. The real gospel demands it. With the focus on faith as participation, there can be no passivity, no being content with merely

10. See also Rom. 3:22; Gal. 3:22; and Phil. 3:9–10.

11. See the classic debate between Richard Hays ("ΠΙΣΤΙΣ [*PISTIS*] and Pauline Christology: What Is at Stake") and James D. G. Dunn ("Once More: ΠΙΣΤΙΣ ΧΡΙΣΤΟΥ [*PISTIS CHRISTOU*]"), in *Society of Biblical Literature 1991 Seminar Papers*, ed. E. H. Lovering Jr. (Atlanta: Scholars Press, 1991), 714–29 and 730–44, respectively. See also Morna D. Hooker, "ΠΙΣΤΙΣ ΧΡΙΣΤΟΥ [*PISTIS CHRISTOU*]," *New Testament Studies* 35 (1989): 321–42.

12. Morgan, *Roman Faith and Christian Faith*, 272–73, 290–91; and David J. Downs and Benjamin J. Lappenga, *The Faithfulness of the Risen Christ: Pistis and the Exalted Lord in the Pauline Letters* (Waco: Baylor University Press, 2019), 3, 21.

thinking right doctrines, and no acting in ways that are an embarrassment to the name of Christ. People need to look in the mirror and be honest about the gospel and its impact. Christ cannot be a mere add-on to our lives.

Is Faith Really about Participation?

Without question, faith is about participation, and the real question is why we, in the contemporary church, have so much focus on Jesus being in our hearts. I provide here an initial look at Paul's thought, but later I will provide a more detailed treatment of participation in various parts of Scripture.

In Paul the emphasis is *much* more on our being in Christ than on his being in us. Paul has 164 occurrences of the Greek equivalents of "in Christ" and related expressions such as "in the Lord," "in him," or "in whom" (referring to Christ). Not all those occurrences should be translated "in," for the Greek preposition *en* can be translated in other ways. Prepositions are notoriously flexible. Still, many of those 164 occurrences mean "*in* Christ." They are "local" in significance, as if Christ were a place! This is the language Paul frequently uses to emphasize how closely faith binds one to Christ. On the other hand, Paul has only five occurrences of Christ in us,[13] or six, depending on how one understands Colossians 1:27.[14] Other texts also point to God's presence in us, such as with temple imagery. For example, 1 Corinthians 3:16 and 6:19 speak of the Holy Spirit dwelling within us; the temple in 3:16 is corporate, and in 6:19 it is individual. Still, the heavy preponderance in Paul's thinking is by far on our being *in Christ*.

Paul understands Christian existence and all the benefits Christ gives as *residing in Christ*. All the good things like grace, love, life,

13. Romans 8:10; 2 Cor. 13:5; Gal. 2:20; 4:19; Eph. 3:17.
14. Does this verse mean "Christ in you the hope of glory" or "Christ among you [gentiles] the hope of glory"? Many scholars argue for the latter because of the context in the letter.

peace—and even election—are found in Christ and are available *only* there. For example, note the following verses:

Romans 6:23: "For the wages of sin is death, but the gift of God is eternal life *in Christ Jesus our Lord.*"

1 Corinthians 1:30: "And from him [God] you are *in Christ Jesus.*"

2 Corinthians 5:17: "So then, if anyone is *in Christ*, new creation has occurred! Old things have passed away; new things have come into being."

Philippians 3:9–10: ". . . that I might be found *in him*, not having my own righteousness from the law but one through the faithfulness of Christ, the righteousness from God based on faith,[15] so that I might know him and the power of his resurrection and *participation* [*koinōnia*] with his sufferings, being conformed to his death."

Colossians 1:2: "To the ones set apart [literally "the holy ones"] and the faithful brothers and sisters *in Christ* in Colossae"— a powerful and profound double geography.

Colossians 2:6–10: "As you received Christ Jesus the Lord, live *in him*, rooted and built up *in him.* . . . And you have been made full *in him.*"

Colossians 3:1, 3: "If then you were *raised with Christ*, seek the things above. . . . For you died, and *your life is hidden with Christ in God.*"

Dozens of such texts could be listed. In the six chapters of Ephesians, Paul has thirty-six occurrences of *en Christō* ("in Christ")

---

15. The translation reflects the breadth of the Greek word *pistis*, which can convey both "faithfulness" and "faith," and also the debate about the meaning of *pistis Christou* (see p. 15). Does the first occurrence in v. 9 mean "the faithfulness of Christ" in his death and resurrection, as I have translated, or does it refer to human faith, as the second occurrence of *pistis* in v. 9 does and as the NIV and NRSV have it?

and related expressions, twenty-three of them in the first two chapters. In English translations not all the occurrences are rendered as "in," but beyond question, Paul views Christian existence as being *in Christ*.

When Paul refers to himself or to other Christians or to their work, he often uses "in Christ" or "in the Lord" as a description. In Romans 16:3 he refers to Prisca and Aquila as his "co-workers *in Christ Jesus*." In 16:7 Andronicus and Junia are described as having been "*in Christ*" before Paul was, in 16:8 Ampliatus is Paul's "beloved *in the Lord*," in 16:9 Urbanus is "our co-worker *in Christ*," and in 16:12 Tryphaena, Tryphosa, and Persis are all said to have "labored *in the Lord*." Among other things, Paul tells people their labor is not useless *in the Lord* (1 Cor. 15:58), and he urges people to be strong *in the Lord* (Eph. 6:10) and to rejoice *in the Lord* (Phil. 3:1). Strikingly, in 2 Corinthians 12:2, Paul refers to his visionary experience by saying, "I know a man *in Christ* who fourteen years ago was caught up to the third heaven—whether *in the body* I do not know or out of the body I do not know; God knows." For Paul, being in Christ is just as much a reality as being in the body.

This is just the way Paul thinks about Christian existence. He has a "spheres of influence" theology,[16] or, if you will, a force-field theology, which involves the notion of an arena constantly controlled by a strong power. A person either lives in and is determined by sin, the flesh, and the world, or one lives in Christ, the Spirit, and even God. The expressions "in the Spirit" or "in God" are less frequent in Paul's writing, with the former occurring only nineteen times and the latter only seven.[17] Being in Christ and being in the Spirit are closely associated, especially as they relate to Christian living, but they are not the same. "In the Spirit" is

16. See Klyne Snodgrass, "Spheres of Influence: A Possible Solution to the Problem of Paul and the Law," *Journal for the Study of the New Testament* 32 (1988): 93–113.
17. "In God" occurs in Rom. 2:17 (of Jews boasting in God); 5:11; Eph. 3:9; Col. 3:3; 1 Thess. 1:1; 2:2; and 2 Thess. 1:1. Note that Jude 1 calls believers people who are loved in God, but the expression is more in keeping with John than Paul.

not used in association with the cross, and Paul could not direct people to be filled with Christ the way he urges them to be filled with the Spirit (Eph. 5:18). Both "in Christ" and "in the Lord" are used in descriptions of people, but while there are exceptions, "in Christ" is used more in statements about salvation and "in the Lord" is used more of Christian actions. "In the Lord" is not used as "in Christ" is to designate the corporate existence of Christians. Still, all of Christian existence is conceived of as in Christ Jesus. Christ is the relation that determines everything.

Clearly, for Paul, *where* one lives determines one's life, actions, and identity. *Geography* is identity, and a Christian's true geography is *in Christ Jesus*.[18] Christ is the believer's new environment. Christianity is a religion that focuses on *participation* in Christ's suffering, death, resurrection life, and glory. Life with Christ cannot be reduced to doctrine about Christ. To be joined to Christ is to be identified with and reproduce in our own lives the two overwhelming events of Christ's death and resurrection. Dying and rising with Christ is at the heart of "in Christ" thinking.

In 1 Corinthians 1:9 Paul writes, "God is faithful, through whom you were called into *participation* [*koinōnia*] with his Son, Jesus Christ our Lord." Often, translations use "fellowship" here instead of "participation," but that seems to trivialize the idea into something more like a church potluck. Paul means being joined to Christ and drawing life from him.[19] Later, in 1 Corinthians 10:16, Paul uses the same word, *koinōnia*, to refer to the partaking of "the cup of blessing" (the wine) and the bread in

18. See Klyne Snodgrass, *Who God Says You Are* (Grand Rapids: Eerdmans, 2018), 14–15, 25, 38, 100, 145–47.

19. See John Calvin in a letter to Peter Martyr Vermigli (August 8, 1555) concerning 1 Cor. 1:9: "The word 'Fellowship' or 'Society' does not sufficiently express his [Paul's] mind. In my judgment, he designates that sacred unity by which the Son of God engrafts us into His body." *Joannis Calvini opera quae supersunt omnia*, ed. Guilielmus Baum, Eduardüs Cunitz, and Eduardus Reuss (Brunswick: O. A. Schwetsohke et Filium, 1876), 15:723, quoted in Julie Canlis, "The Geography of Participation: *In Christ* Is Location, Location, Location," *Ex Auditu* 33 (2017): 130–46, here 137n40.

the Lord's Supper and says the partaking is a participation in his blood (death) and his body. This is no mere happy feeling of getting together but a deep involvement and engagement with all that Christ is. It is union and solidarity with Christ and all he has done and is doing. Faith in Christ, then, is a "Christ intimacy," as an earlier scholar put it,[20] a relation that rearranges and redirects life.

I have focused initially on Paul, but obviously the Johannine writings focus on participation just as much, even if a bit differently. Here there is the reciprocal idea of our *remaining* in Christ (or God) and his remaining in us, especially in John 15 and 1 John 2–4. This language of remaining in Christ is an emphatic focus on participation with Christ. Even here the focus is more on our remaining in Christ than on Christ being in us. We will return to the Johannine material below.

Without question, the gospel is a gospel of participation. It is first of all about God's participation with us and secondly about our participation with God. God's participation is seen in the love of God, the incarnation, the death and resurrection of Jesus, and the giving of the Spirit. Our participation means being *joined* to Christ in faith. That does not mean merely participating in doing things; it means participating in the life in Christ or in God, or, better, *participating in the life of Christ and of God through the Spirit and being transformed by the participation*. It is about drawing our identity from our close participation with the triune God.

Is this outrageous? As we will see, it was not for the early church or for the church down through the ages. Although Paul does not use language of participating in the triune God, he lays the foundation for it with his use of "in Christ," "in the Spirit," and "in God." And John Calvin found the idea of participation with God already included in the Genesis account of creation in the

---

20. Adolph Deissmann, *Paul: A Study in Social and Religious History*, trans. William E. Wilson, 2nd ed. (New York: Doran, n.d.), 152.

image of God.[21] Rather than being outrageous, such participation is the driving concern of all Scripture.

Participation Is Foundational for Theology and Ethics

Participation thinking enables theological understanding, especially in a Christology emphasizing the incarnation—God with us and participating with us. Early Christians knew that in Jesus Christ they encountered an unparalleled revelation of God. This conviction was primarily a result of the resurrection. If Jesus Christ is the resurrected Lord, if God created life in the midst of death, if Jesus's death was viewed as God's identification with humanity, and if, as risen Lord, Jesus was understood to be the giver of life through God's Spirit, then it is not difficult to transition to the thought of people being in some way bonded to him, which broadened their understanding even more of who he is. Obviously early Christians had taken an enormous step in their thinking about Jesus the Christ. How did they so quickly revamp their thinking so that they could say regarding a man, whom some of them knew and with whom they recently had been walking around, whose brothers and sisters they knew, that the lives of all believers and indeed all things were *in him*? To them he was no mere mortal human. The relevance of participation for Christology must not be neglected.

Participation is equally important with reference to salvation/ atonement and ethics. In fact, the failure of people to deal with participation language has caused numerous problems, including sterile and abstract views of faith that treat it as if it were about mere thinking, suggestions that justification is legal fiction (God knows you are guilty but says you are innocent anyway), an insufficient basis for ethics (why be ethical if you are already declared

21. See John Calvin, *Institutes of the Christian Religion*, trans. Ford Lewis Battles, 2 vols., Library of Christian Classics 20 (Philadelphia: Westminster, 1960), 2.1.5 and 2.2.1.

righteous?), and difficulty in explaining atonement ideas. Just why and what does the death of a Jew long ago have anything to do with us? It does not unless there is some *solidarity* with Christ and some participation in his very being, which is what faith is about. Apart from participation, faith starts to look like a human work. Have I believed enough and accurately enough? And then there is the really life-changing part: participation compels ethics, for ethics flow directly from participation with Christ. We will revisit atonement ideas and ethics when treating specific texts in Paul's Letters.

Clearly, any thought of salvation as less than complete association with Christ cannot be true faith in Christ. Therefore, any proclamation of the gospel that does not result in *participation with Christ and God by the Spirit* cannot be an adequate explanation of the gospel. This solidarity extends to *thought, word, and actions*. The result of the gospel and the essence of Christianity are about being attached to Jesus so that you draw life from him, are shaped by his character, and are engaged in his concerns. That is the real gospel we all need.

Participation thinking is the assumption of so much else in the New Testament. For example, we are told to pray all the time, continually (1 Thess. 5:17; Eph. 6:18). How can anyone do that and live? The instruction to pray without ceasing does not mean being on your knees and always praying. It calls for an awareness of participation with God, awareness that one's life is always engaged with God and is always in communication with God. Life is lived before and with God.

Don't Let It Go to Your Head

A warning is in order, for any emphasis can be wrongly grasped. With participation there are dangers, such as the spiritual arrogance evident at Corinth and delusions of perfectionism, but such perversions only show that people did not or do not understand participation at all. Paul's solution to the problems is to keep reminding people of the gospel's emphasis on who they are in Christ. There is no solution to the church's problems other than the continual application of the gospel of participation. Also, for all the language about participating with God, or, as 2 Peter 1:4 has it, partaking of the divine nature, we do not become God or the same as God.[22] This is not like apotheosis in Roman thought, in which the Caesars became gods at their death.[23] It is not some type of mysticism. It is not about ontology, taking on God's being, his essence. It is not being parallel to God or being God; it is *ongoing engagement with God* as people created in God's image for relation to God. It involves no loss of individuality, for true individuality is enhanced where life is engaged and experienced, not merely observed. Union with God is a "differentiated union, one that does not annihilate the clear distinction between Creator and creature."[24]

Participation is about sharing in God's *moral* character because of a close relation to God and drawing life from God. It is *not* true that *everything* about the person changes because of participation with Christ. Many individual and cultural characteristics may remain the same,[25] but everything about our identity as individuals is subjected to and filtered by Christ. Despite the dangers of misunderstanding, the benefits of participation far outweigh the liabilities. No other gospel exists apart from the

22. There is evidence, however, that some had this in mind. See, e.g., Justin, *Dialogue with Trypho* 124, in *Ante-Nicene Fathers*, ed. Alexander Roberts and James Donaldson (repr., Peabody, MA: Hendrickson, 1994), 1:262: "The Holy Ghost reproaches men because they were made like God; . . . yet thereby it is demonstrated that all men are deemed worthy of becoming 'gods,' and of having power to become sons of the Highest."

23. Vespasian reportedly said on his deathbed, "I think I am becoming a god." Suetonius, *Vespasian* 23, in *Lives of the Caesars*, 2 vols., trans. J. C. Rolfe, Loeb Classical Library (Cambridge, MA: Harvard University Press, 1979), 2:319.

24. J. Todd Billings, *Union with Christ: Reframing Theology and Ministry for the Church* (Grand Rapids: Baker Academic, 2011), 64.

25. See William S. Campbell, *Paul and the Creation of Christian Identity* (London: T&T Clark, 2008), esp. 54–66.

gospel of participation with and in Christ, and this is the gospel we all need.

The following chapters will discuss the gospel of participation in more detail. As far as I know, scholars have not treated participation much outside the Pauline and Johannine writings. I will show participation is part of nearly all of Scripture, even if it is presented in a variety of ways. First, however, I need to show that salvation as participation has always been the teaching of the church.

two

Is Faith as Participation a New Idea?

Nearly all great Christian thinkers have focused on participation.

Stephen Chester[1]

Rather than being a novel idea, salvation as participation is a long-held emphasis that, unfortunately, the modern church has mostly lost. Biblical scholars, especially those focusing on Paul's Letters, have always known about participation and union with Christ. The gulf between discussions in academic studies of the New Testament and popular discussions, including those conducted by some pastors, is enormous. Scholars may sometimes be part of the problem, but not here. Over many years, major scholars—including Adolf Deissmann, Albert Schweitzer, James Stewart, D. E. H. Whiteley, E. P. Sanders, and many more—have just assumed that, for Paul, Christian faith *is* participation in Christ.[2]

1. Private conversation with the author.
2. Adolf Deissmann, *Paul: A Study in Social and Religious History*, trans. William E. Wilson, 2nd ed. (New York: Doran, n.d.; the German first edition was published in 1925); Albert Schweitzer, *The Mysticism of Paul the Apostle*, trans. William Montgomery (London: Black, 1931); James Stewart, *A Man in Christ: The Vital Elements of St. Paul's Religion* (New York: Harper, 1935); D. E. H. Whiteley, *The Theology of*

Long before Sanders brought renewed attention to participation with his 1977 publication *Paul and Palestinian Judaism*, Whiteley in 1964 wrote, "If St. Paul can be said to hold a theory of the *modus operandi* [of atonement], it is best described as one of salvation through participation: Christ shared all our experiences, sin alone excepted, including death, in order that we, by virtue of our solidarity with him, might share his life."[3] More recently, Michael Gorman has written, "Participation is not merely one aspect of Pauline theology and spirituality, or a supplement to something more fundamental; rather, it is at the very heart of Paul's thinking and living. Pauline soteriology is inherently participatory and transformative."[4]

But it is not just Paul. It is all of Scripture and all of church history. Todd Billings, writing on Calvin, says, "Union with Christ is theological shorthand for the gospel itself,"[5] and Kevin Vanhoozer similarly says, "'In Christ' is shorthand for the whole doctrine of salvation, and thus the whole of redemptive history."[6] Biblical faith cannot be understood apart from ideas of union, attachment, and participation. *Faith is a real participation with Christ.* Faith has an adhesive quality to it; it *attaches* you to Jesus Christ.

Nor is it just modern biblical scholars and theologians who focus on participation. *Nearly all* great Christian thinkers throughout

---

St. Paul (Philadelphia: Fortress, 1964); and E. P. Sanders, *Paul and Palestinian Judaism: A Comparison of Patterns of Religion* (Philadelphia: Fortress, 1977).

3. Whiteley, *Theology of St. Paul*, 130, also 134, 147. Whiteley's explanation of participation is not clear enough.

4. Michael Gorman, "Paul's Corporate, Cruciform, Missional *Theosis* in 2 Corinthians," in *"In Christ" in Paul: Explorations in Paul's Theology of Union and Participation*, ed. Michael J. Thate, Kevin J. Vanhoozer, and Constantine R. Campbell, Wissenschaftliche Untersuchungen zum Neuen Testament 2/384 (Tübingen: Mohr Siebeck, 2014), 181–208, here 181.

5. J. Todd Billings, *Union with Christ: Reframing Theology and Ministry for the Church* (Grand Rapids: Baker Academic, 2011), 1.

6. Kevin Vanhoozer, "From 'Blessed in Christ' to 'Being in Christ': The State of Union and the Place of Participation in Paul's Discourse, New Testament Exegesis, and Systematic Theology Today," in Thate, Vanhoozer, and Campbell, *"In Christ" in Paul*, 3–33, here 17.

the church's history have focused on participation.[7] As a sampling, notice the following (the italics in the quotations are mine):[8]

Clement of Rome (AD 95): "And is it any wonder that *those who in Christ* were entrusted by God with such a work appointed the leaders just mentioned?" (*1 Clement* 43.1).

Ignatius (c. 110): ". . . in order that he may . . . *acknowledge that you are members [melē] of his Son. It is, therefore, advantageous for you to be in perfect unity, in order that you may always have a share in [metechēte] God*" (Ignatius, *To the Ephesians* 4.2). This is an early and powerful statement. In 9.2 believers are called "God-bearers, temple-bearers, Christ-bearers." This is not "thinking about God and Christ"; this is serious engagement with God and Christ.

Epistle of Barnabas (c. 120) 3.6: ". . . the people whom he had prepared *in his Beloved*."

Martyrdom of Polycarp (c. 155?) 6.2: "The captain of the police . . . was eager to bring him into the stadium in order that he [Polycarp] might fulfill his appointed destiny of being made a *sharer with Christ [Christou koinōnos genomenos]*."

Irenaeus (c. 180): "He caused man (human nature) *to cleave to and to become one with God.* . . . And unless man had been *joined to God*, he never could have become a *partaker* of incorruptibility" (*Against Heresies* 3.18.7). He also says, " . . . our Lord Jesus Christ, who did, through his transcendent love, become what we are, that He might bring us to be even what He is Himself" (*Against Heresies* 5, preface).[9] This

---

7. My colleague Stephen Chester first made this point to me in conversation. For a treatment of patristic views on participation and other representatives, see Grant Macaskill, *Union with Christ in the New Testament* (Oxford: Oxford University Press, 2013), 42–76.

8. The translations of the first four items are from *The Apostolic Fathers in English*, trans. and ed. Michael W. Holmes, 3rd ed. (Grand Rapids: Baker Academic, 2006).

9. Irenaeus, *Against Heresies*, in *Ante-Nicene Fathers*, ed. Alexander Roberts and James Donaldson (repr., Peabody, MA: Hendrickson, 1994), 1:448, 526.

foundational idea is repeated often throughout the church's history as a summary of the Christian faith.

Athanasius (c. 357): *"By participation of the Spirit, we are knit into the Godhead"* (*Orations against the Arians* 3.24).[10] Such an astounding statement from one of the most important theologians of the church must not be ignored.

Gregory of Nyssa (c. 375): "But, 'the Mediator between God and men' who through Himself *joins the human being to God* connects to God only that which is worthy of *union with Him*. For just as He in Himself assimilated His own human nature to the power of the Godhead, . . . so, also, will He lead each person to *union with the Godhead*. . . . But, if anyone is truly 'the temple of God,' . . . this person is *given a share in the Godhead by the Mediator*" (*On Perfection*).[11] This work, which describes the Christian life, is riddled with participation ideas and uses at least a dozen different Greek words to convey ideas of union with Christ and having a share in Christ.

Augustine (c. 398): "Therefore, I would not exist—I would simply not be at all—unless I exist in thee [God], from whom and by whom and in whom all things are" (*Confessions* 1.2),[12] and "It is God who is blessed in himself and also makes us blessed, and, *because he became a participant in our humanity, he provided a shortcut to participation in his divinity*" (*City of God* 9.15).[13]

Thomas Aquinas (c. 1270): "Now the gift of grace surpasses every capacity of created nature, since it is nothing other

10. Athanasius, *Orations against the Arians*, in *Nicene and Post-Nicene Fathers*, series 2, ed. Philip Schaff and Henry Wace (repr., Peabody, MA: Hendrickson, 1994), 4:407.

11. Saint Gregory of Nyssa, *Ascetical Works*, trans. Virginia Woods Callahan, The Fathers of the Church, A New Translation (Washington, DC: Catholic University of America Press, 1967), 116.

12. Augustine, *Confessions and Enchiridion*, trans. Albert C. Outler, Library of Christian Classics 7 (Philadelphia: Westminster, 1955), 32.

13. Augustine, *The City of God*, trans. William Babcock, The Works of Saint Augustine I/6 (Hyde Park, NY: New City, 2012). See also *City of God* 21.15; and *Expositions of the Psalms* on Ps. 122:3.

than *a certain participation in the divine nature, which surpasses every other nature. . . . So it is* necessary that God alone should make godlike, *by communicating a share in his divine nature by participation and assimilation"* (*Summa Theologiæ* I-II, question 112, article 1).[14]

Martin Luther (1535): "Therefore Christian faith is not an idle quality or an empty husk in the heart. . . . *It takes hold of Christ* in such a way that Christ is the object of faith, or rather not the object but . . . *the One who is present in the faith itself. . . . Therefore faith justifies because it takes hold of and possesses this treasure, the present Christ"* (*Lectures on Galatians 1535*, at 2:16).[15] Luther repeatedly emphasizes that faith takes hold of Christ. For example, he adds, "Faith takes hold of Christ and has him present, enclosing him as the ring encloses the gem" (p. 132). He then explains, "But faith must be taught correctly, namely, that by it you are so *cemented* to Christ that He and you are as one person, which cannot be separated but remains attached to Him forever and declares: 'I am as Christ'" (p. 168). In his *The Freedom of a Christian* he adds, *"[A] Christian lives not in himself, but in Christ and in his neighbor. Otherwise he is not a Christian."*[16] Given these statements from Luther and those of Calvin that follow, George Hunsinger's words are not surprising: "Faith as participation . . . is the very heartbeat of the Reformation. It is the key to the doctrine of justification by faith alone."[17]

14. Thomas Aquinas, *The Gospel of Grace*, trans. Cornelius Ernst, vol. 30 of *Summa Theologiæ*, Blackfrairs ed. (New York: McGraw Hill, 1972), 145–47.

15. Martin Luther, *Lectures on Galatians 1535: Chapters 1–4*, ed. Jaroslav Pelikan and Walter A. Hansen, trans. Jaroslav Pelikan, Luther's Works 26 (St. Louis: Concordia, 1963), 129–30.

16. Martin Luther, *The Freedom of a Christian*, in *Career of the Reformer I*, ed. Harold J. Grimm, trans. W. A. Lambert and Harold J. Grimm, Luther's Works 31 (Philadelphia: Fortress, 1957), 371.

17. See George Hunsinger, *"Fides Christo Formata*: Luther, Barth, and the Joint Declaration," in *The Gospel of Justification in Christ: Where Does the Church Stand Today?*, ed. Wayne C. Stumme (Grand Rapids: Eerdmans, 2006), 69–84, here 75.

John Calvin (1536): "*As long as Christ remains outside of us, and we are separated from him, all that he has suffered and done for the salvation of the human race remains useless and of no value for us.* Therefore, to share with us what he has received from the Father, he had to become ours and to dwell within us. . . . *We also, in turn, are said to be 'engrafted into him' and to 'put on Christ'; for, as I have said, all that he possesses is nothing to us until we grow into one body with him*" (*Institutes of the Christian Religion* 3.11.10).[18]

Katharina von Bora (1552), Martin Luther's wife, is reported to have said on her deathbed, "I will stick to Christ as a burr to cloth." Some think the statement is instead from Katharina of Saxony, but regardless of the origin, this one is my favorite![19]

Westminster Larger Catechism (1647) 65–90 describes all of salvation as union and communion with Christ in grace and glory.

John Wesley (c. 1755): "In baptism we, through faith, are *ingrafted into Christ*; and we draw new spiritual life from this new root through his Spirit, who fashions us like unto him, and particularly with regard to his death and resurrection" (*Wesley's Notes on the Bible*, on Rom. 6:3).[20]

These people were serious about the fact that faith in Christ means being *taken into the life of Christ and replicating that life in the way one lives*. Others could easily be listed, such as Cyril of Alexandria, Anselm,[21] John Owen, the Mercersburg theology of

18. John Calvin, *Institutes of the Christian Religion*, trans. Ford Lewis Battles, 2 vols., Library of Christian Classics 20 (Philadelphia: Westminster, 1960), 3.1.1. See also 3.11.10.

19. See the discussion by Matthew Carver, "The 'Klette' Hymns and the 'Klette' Quote," *Hymnoglypt* (blog), May 1, 2010, https://matthaeusglyptes.blogspot.com /2010/05/klette-hymns-and-klette-quote.html.

20. John Wesley, *Wesley's Notes on the Bible*, ed. G. Roger Schoenhals (Grand Rapids: Francis Asbury, 1987), 500.

21. See Karl Barth's comment (*Anselm: Fides Quaerens Intellectum*, trans. Ian W. Robertson [London: SCM, 1960], 17): "For Anselm, 'to believe' does not mean simply

the nineteenth century, and Karl Barth and Thomas F. Torrance[22] in the twentieth, to mention only a few. One analysis of participation in Barth's theology asserts, "Revelation, election, creation, reconciliation, and redemption all take place in Christ, and their meaning and content may be rightly apprehended only in him. *The creature is incorporated into a depth of fellowship that is nothing less than participation in the being of God. . . . Participation belongs at the fundamental core of Barth's theology, is present in one way or another in virtually every part of* Church Dogmatics, *and is essential for understanding the work as a whole.*"[23]

Imagine the impact that would result if Christians took seriously participation in the being of God. Some church liturgies retain words about union with Christ, even if any understanding of participation as something central and lived, actually determining life, is hard to find. Certainly, too, a focus on union and participation has caused debate and disagreement among theologians, including Calvin and Luther. I cannot, and make no attempt to, do justice to the history of the discussions of participation, but Scripture over and over, in text after text after text, emphasizes participation, and the church's history does too. *Nearly all great Christian thinkers have emphasized participation.* Why don't we?

People rightly complain about the fractures in and disunity among Christian denominations, but surely, as diverse as these traditions are, participation is *one ground for unity in the church*, and a massive one at that. This is important! Theologians of all stripes affirm that participation with Christ is what Christianity is about. But the nagging question is this: if patristic scholars,

---

a striving of the human will towards God, but a striving of the human will *into God, and so a participation . . . in God's mode of Being and so a similar participation in God's aseity,* in the matchless glory of his very Self, and therefore also in God's utter absence of necessity" (italics mine).

22. See Geordie W. Ziegler, *Trinitarian Grace and Participation: An Entry into the Theology of T. F. Torrance* (Minneapolis: Fortress, 2017).

23. Adam Neder, *Participation in Christ: An Entry into Karl Barth's "Church Dogmatics,"* Columbia Series in Reformed Theology (Louisville: Westminster John Knox, 2009), xi, xii (italics mine).

the Reformers, and modern biblical scholars and theologians all know and emphasize participation, why is it so seldom heard in the church?

Why Has the Focus on Participation Been Lost?

Over several years I posed this question to a number of scholars but did not receive a satisfactory answer.[24] Suggested ways of accounting for the loss include a number of options: (1) the sense of individualism resulting from the Enlightenment; (2) the loss of theological tradition, which is surely a factor; (3) other agendas dominating after World War I; (4) too heavy of an emphasis on justification language and ideas of imputation, which separated justification from sanctification; (5) the inability to translate the idea meaningfully; and (6) the focus in the Great Awakenings and evangelistic movements on decision. All of these suggestions may be contributing factors, but none is fully convincing. When I asked one of my classes why this emphasis had been lost, one young woman, perceiving the implications of participation, responded, "Perhaps the cost is too high." Ouch! We would prefer some act we could perform and then get on with our lives as we wish. The cost of participation ideas is high, if you want to go your own way, but the benefits are even higher if you dare to take this gospel seriously. What could be greater than life bound to God, the source of life and all goodness?

Søren Kierkegaard and Participation

One other voice deserves to be mentioned, and I will quote him occasionally in the rest of this book. Søren Kierkegaard, to my knowledge, does not actually use the language of participation,

24. I draw here on my article "The Gospel of Participation," in *Earliest Christianity within the Boundaries of Judaism: Essays in Honor of Bruce Chilton*, ed. Alan J. Avery-Peck, Craig A. Evans, and Jacob Neusner (Leiden: Brill, 2016), 413–30.

but it well summarizes his concerns. He does speak of being joined
to Christ in order to imitate him and of life being continually lived
before God.[25] Kierkegaard is known for his attack on Christendom
and the failure of people to take Christianity seriously. His complaints are justified and searing. Something similar is needed in our
time, but not as an attack on the Christendom Kierkegaard knew,
for Christendom no longer exists. With Christendom everyone
assumed a Christian substructure and assumed they were Christians. Now most in our society do not care about Christianity at
all; some assume they belong in some way to the Christian faith,
but the church and its message have relatively little impact.

In his *Practice in Christianity* Kierkegaard repeatedly emphasizes *being contemporaneous* with Christ, rigorousness, earnestness, being continually under examination by God, and being a
follower of Christ and not merely an admirer. He takes Christianity seriously, but then, can anyone legitimately take Christianity lightly? *There is no Christianity lite.* In articulating his
concerns, Kierkegaard describes much that is intended with
participation. For example, being contemporaneous with Christ
emphasizes closeness to Christ and will not allow distance in
geography or length of time to detract from the impact of the
presence of Christ. Being continually under examination by God
keeps engagement with and awareness of our responsibility to
God front and center. We live our lives with and participate with
the God revealed in Jesus Christ.

Our problems are not Kierkegaard's. He fought against nineteenth-century Danish Christendom, where everyone was presumed
to be a Christian. Our problems are more serious, but the solution
in Kierkegaard's time and in ours is the same—actually embrac-
ing what the biblical message is about. Faith as participation is the

25. See Søren Kierkegaard, *Practice in Christianity*, ed. and trans. Howard V. Hong
and Edna H. Hong, Kierkegaard's Writings 20 (Princeton: Princeton University Press,
1991), 237; and Kierkegaard, *Sickness unto Death: A Christian Psychological Exposi-
tion for Upbuilding and Awakening*, ed. and trans. Howard V. Hong and Edna H.
Hong, Kierkegaard's Writings 19 (Princeton: Princeton University Press, 1980), 83, 85.

solution we need for living, both for those claiming the faith and those who think it is irrelevant.

Whatever else is said, clearly participation is not some new fad. It has always been the assumption of the meaning of faith from the New Testament on and with nearly all great Christian thinkers.

three

What Is Participation, and Why Is It Important?

Nothing is more dangerous to true Christianity, nothing more contrary to its nature, than to get [people] to assume light-mindedly the name of Christian.

Søren Kierkegaard[1]

If the church's great thinkers throughout history have focused on participation, in recent years there has been an explosion of publications emphasizing participation with Christ.[2] *Numerous* studies on participation in the New Testament, church history, and theology have appeared, as a glance at the select bibliography below shows. And there have been numerous reevaluations of the meaning of *pistis* ("faith/faithfulness") and of the phrase *pistis Christou* ("the faith/faithfulness of Christ").[3]

1. Søren Kierkegaard, *Kierkegaard's Attack upon "Christendom," 1854–1855,* trans. Walter Lowrie (Princeton: Princeton University Press, 1946), 84.

2. E. P. Sanders's *Paul and Palestinian Judaism: A Comparison of Patterns of Religion* (Philadelphia: Fortress, 1977) was a catalyst for much of this renewed emphasis, but many earlier studies existed.

3. Most recently, David J. Downs and Benjamin J. Lappenga, *The Faithfulness of the Risen Christ: Pistis and the Exalted Lord in the Pauline Letters* (Waco: Baylor University Press, 2019). See p. 15, and particularly n. 11.

For a long time, and still with some, the language of participation was set against the language of justification/righteousness. People debated which was foundational, but that debate is unfortunate. Both ideas are crucial, as are other terms, such as "reconciliation," "new creation," "rebirth," "being set apart," and the like. These terms do not need to be set against each other. With all such terms the early church strained to describe a reality words are too impoverished to convey, but with all of the terms, participation is explicit or assumed. The truth is that *justification, and any other act of salvation, happens only because of participation in Christ and his work*, and several texts show that. For example, Galatians 2:17 says, "But if seeking to be justified *in Christ* . . ." (see also Rom. 3:24; 1 Cor. 1:30; and Phil. 3:9). Every benefit of the Christian faith is found *in Christ*—and nowhere else.

But if participation ideas are so important, what is participation, and why is it so important? We can acknowledge that we will never grasp all the richness of participation, but it is not some mystery that defies understanding. The first thing that must be said is that participation does not start with us humans. *God chooses to participate with us.* God is for us. God's initiative in participation is *overwhelmingly* primary and is most evident in the incarnation, in the pouring out of the love of God in the death and resurrection of Christ, and in the pouring out of the Holy Spirit. Also, the ongoing participation of God in our lives is evident in the work of the Spirit, who leads, convicts, transforms, and empowers Christians every day.

Obviously, too, the human side of participation involves the participation of the Holy Spirit. We do nothing by ourselves. God is at work, drawing us and enabling faith. "Prevenient grace," the grace that comes before grace, is the label often given to God's work in us before we are even aware of it. Participation presupposes an engagement of God with humans at every stage of the process. But *you* must act. Augustine said, "God made you without you. . . . He doesn't justify you without you."[4] How do we do justice to the relation between God's sovereignty and human response, to the focus on salvation being totally the work of God but one in which we are totally engaged? Scripture does not fully answer this question, but participation takes us a *long* way in the discussion. As we will see, there are resources, especially in the Old Testament and in the book of Acts, for dealing with such issues.

Whatever the explanation, the gospel does not seek a less robust focus on the individual. *You* must act. But the gospel seeks something additional, equally important, much larger, almost beyond understanding: the realization that you live in God/Christ and are not merely an individual. By faith you are joined to Christ and draw life from him. Can this be true? Does life have meaning otherwise?

How Literal Is Participation Language?

Is participation language merely a "subjective" idea, so that one *feels* in union with Christ? Is it something merely mental? Albert Schweitzer and Alfred Wikenhauser, two of the earlier scholars to recover the emphasis on participation, rejected this possibility, as have many others. They argued there is something real, something "objective" about the union, saying baptism creates an objective reality.[5] But what in the world does "objective" mean in such use? Certainly participation is mental, for it involves an outlook about life that must be implemented, but it is more than thinking right thoughts. It is about the whole of life, actions and all else, being *housed* in Christ's life. Participation is not merely about imitation

4. Augustine, *Sermons*, vol. 5, *148–183*, trans. Edmund Hill, ed. John E. Rotelle, The Works of Saint Augustine III/5 (New Rochelle, NY: New City, 1992), 169.13.

5. Albert Schweitzer, *The Mysticism of Paul the Apostle*, trans. William Montgomery (London: Black, 1931), 117, 125, 127, 139; and Alfred Wikenhauser, *Pauline Mysticism: Christ in the Mystical Teaching of St. Paul*, trans. Joseph Cunningham (New York: Herder & Herder, 1960), 102–5.

of Christ but about identification with him and union with him. "Putting on Christ" (Gal. 3:27) involves more than thinking about Christ, which is presumably what people mean when they say life in Christ is not merely subjective; it means that all of life is determined by Christ.

Further, what does union with Christ or being in Christ (*en Christō*) really mean? It is not literally, physically true. Obviously, being in Christ and participation with Christ are metaphors, but they are not "merely metaphors," as if "metaphor" meant less than real. Metaphor often expresses a reality that literal language cannot convey. Participation language describes a reality that cannot be brushed off as a pious thought. Metaphorical it may be, but the reality is that Christ is the environment in which people of faith live. This is what Christianity is about—a oneness with Jesus Christ, a Christ intimacy, that determines life. Consequently, for Paul a favorite metaphor for Christian existence is "the body of Christ" *of which we are members* (see esp. Rom. 12:5 and Eph. 5:30).

Grammatical explanations of the Greek expression *en Christō* ("in Christ"), for all their value, flounder. Granted, some uses of the phrase are instrumental and express agency. Something happens *by* Christ. Other suggestions are offered, such as a causal meaning, in which something would be caused by Christ. Those attempting such explanations admit the categories overlap. The nuance in a given case is sometimes difficult to assess, but without question, many passages are about *location in Christ*, an incorporative union with him.[6] James Dunn says, "Paul evidently felt himself to be caught up 'in Christ' and borne along by Christ. In some sense he experienced Christ as the context of all his being and doing."[7] *That* is what Paul understood as the meaning of faith! That is what participation is about.

6. See the discussion of Murray J. Harris, *Prepositions and Theology in the Greek New Testament: An Essential Reference Resource for Exegesis* (Grand Rapids: Zondervan, 2012), 122–36.

7. James D. G. Dunn, *The Theology of Paul the Apostle* (Grand Rapids: Eerdmans, 1998), 400. See also p. 405: "To be baptized into Christ is complementary to or

We can feel the New Testament authors straining for language that does justice to the reality of life in Christ, and we need to reflect carefully on the variety of ways the language is used. Each text with the expression *en Christō* or something similar must be considered in its own right. Romans 8:1–2 is a good example. In verse 1, "There is now no condemnation to those who are in [*en*] Christ Jesus" *has* to be understood as "local." For those who are joined to Christ, who are one with him, and whose identity is housed in his, there is no condemnation. However, in verse 2 the meaning of *en Christō* is debated and depends on whether *en Christō* connects to "life" and is local in significance or to "freed," which would make it instrumental. In other words, does the text mean "For the law of the Spirit of *life in Christ Jesus* freed you from the law of sin and death," or does it mean "For the law of the Spirit of life *by Christ Jesus* freed you from the law of sin and death"? Either is possible, and both stress the centrality of Christ in salvation.

The attempts of grammarians and translators to explain *en Christō* are frustrating, and people do not agree about specific texts and about the meaning of terms. For example, is the NIV correct in translating Romans 3:24 as "justified . . . through the redemption *that came by* Christ Jesus"? Or would we not be better served by translating the text more straightforwardly as "justified through the redemption *in* Christ Jesus"? Regarding terms, some scholars make distinctions between "union," "participation," "identification," and "incorporation"[8] and find such terms differing in value. I do not find any basis for distinguishing the terms or favoring one above the other. Any of these terms goes well beyond typical language and has in mind such close attachment to Christ that identity and character are *by necessity transformed.*

---

equivalent to assuming the persona of Christ. In both cases some sort of identification or sense of bound-up-with-ness is implicit."

8. See, e.g., Constantine R. Campbell, *Paul and Union with Christ: An Exegetical and Theological Study* (Grand Rapids: Zondervan, 2012), 412–14.

Regarding translation, unless a text is clearly instrumental or causal, if at all possible we will do better to stay with "in" (i.e., local) language so that readers feel the impact of Paul's participation theology.[9]

Regardless of such questions, however, there can be no doubt that participation is at the center of Paul's understanding of our relation with Christ. Dying and rising with Christ, baptism, and the Lord's Supper are all about participation. Dying and rising with Christ summarizes well Paul's understanding of "faith." To believe is to align oneself with Jesus's death and resurrection and to *replicate* that pattern in one's existence. That means, with the help of God's Spirit, one continually dies to / rejects a self-centered, old way of existence dominated by sin and continually rises to / experiences life transformed and energized by God. This focus on dying and rising is dominant in a significant number of texts: Romans 6:1–14; 7:1–6; 8:1–14, 17; 2 Corinthians 4:10–12; 5:14–17; Galatians 2:19–20; 5:24–25; 6:14–15; Ephesians 2:5–8; Philippians 3:9–11; Colossians 2:12–13; and 2:20–3:4. Other texts may not be so explicit in the language of dying and rising, but they carry the same nuance (see Eph. 4:22–24 and Col. 3:9–11).

To take only one example from this list, the well-known words of Galatians 2:19–20 should be taken seriously: "I have been crucified with Christ. *I am no longer living* [!], but Christ lives in me. What I now live in the flesh [in this body] I live by faith in the Son of God, who loved me and gave himself for me." Faith for Paul means that his life is not his own; rather, it belongs to the risen Christ, to whom he is joined. He lives from this Christ intimacy. Or to use the words of Richard Longenecker, "Being 'in Christ' is,

---

9. Paul can use *en* in relation to humans other than Christ: Moses (1 Cor. 10:2); Adam (1 Cor. 15:22); Abraham (Gal. 3:8 via a pronoun in an Old Testament quotation); Isaac (Rom. 9:7, again an Old Testament quotation); Pharaoh (Rom. 9:17 via a pronoun in an Old Testament quotation); Elijah (Rom. 11:2, "in the passage about Elijah"); and "in me" (Phil. 1:30). None of these, apart from Adam, is relevant for understanding participation with Christ. Adam is, at most, a representative figure, and being "in Adam" is only partially analogous to incorporation in Christ.

for Paul, communion with Christ in the most intimate relationship imaginable, without ever destroying or minimizing—rather, only enhancing—the distinctive personalities of either the Christian or Christ. It is 'I-Thou' communion at its highest."[10]

What Is the Origin of This Language?

Asking about the origin of participation thinking helps in understanding the term, even though the origin is debated. Significantly, there is no real parallel in the Greco-Roman world.[11] Yet, participation is simply the character of the God of the Bible, and much of the rest of this book will show that. God is a God who chooses to participate—even if as an elusive presence! More specifically regarding origin as it relates to the Old Testament, scholars point to corporate solidarity,[12] the tabernacle and temple, texts about God dwelling with people, and texts about people residing with God, such as Psalm 90:1 (which says of God, "You have been our dwelling place throughout all generations" [NIV]). These are all significant and demonstrate an awareness that God and his people are intertwined, something often neglected now by many Christians.

From the New Testament, scholars point to Jesus's taking on the task of Israel,[13] his Synoptic teaching on discipleship as

10. Richard N. Longenecker, *Galatians*, Word Biblical Commentary 41 (Dallas: Word, 1990), 154.

11. The closest might be in Seneca, *Epistle* 41.1, and Dio Chrysostom, *Discourses* 12.28. The quotation in Acts 17:28 should be included as well, but there is significant uncertainty about its origin. It is attributed to Epimenides (sixth century BC), but it is preserved only in a much later Syriac Christian father, who may be dependent on earlier Christian material. See the treatment by Craig S. Keener, *Acts: An Exegetical Commentary* (Grand Rapids: Baker Academic, 2014), 3:2657–59.

12. That sense that the nation or group is bound up with the individual and vice versa.

13. N. T. Wright thinks Paul viewed the people of God and the Messiah of God as so bound together that what was true of the one was true of the other. People are incorporated into Jesus, who has taken on the task of Israel. Jesus did take on the task of Israel, but I do not think this is the origin of participation with Christ. Wright's

following him, his teaching on "remaining" in John's Gospel, and texts on the Lord's Supper and baptism. Surely the church's attempt to grasp the meaning of the cross and resurrection is foundational. All these are significant, but baptism and the Lord's Supper are the primary sources for the church's appropriating the cross and resurrection, and therefore, they have to be the source of participation thinking, this new way of conceiving of life and salvation.

In baptism believers are "plunged" into Christ to such a degree it is as if they put on Christ like a garment. This is the language of Galatians 3:26–27: "For you are all children of God through faith in Christ Jesus,[14] for those of you who were baptized into Christ have clothed yourselves with Christ." The same idea of being placed into Christ at baptism is evident in Romans 6:3 ("Or do you not know that we who were baptized into Christ Jesus were baptized into his death?") and 1 Corinthians 12:13 ("For in [or by] one Spirit we were all baptized into one body"). In baptism one takes on a new identity, an identity stamped with the character of the crucified and risen Lord. Cross-shaped baptistries that ringed the Mediterranean from the fourth to the sixth centuries demonstrated the theology well. (See the striking picture from Mamshit in the Negev of Israel.) People took their baptismal identity standing in the middle of the cross. They understood what participation was about!

The Lord's Supper is equally a source for participation thinking, as is obvious from the "ingesting" language of the words of

---

suggestion that the background for "in Christ" is the words "We have no portion *in David*, no share *in the son of Jesse*" (2 Sam. 20:1; 1 Kings 12:16) is without merit. The text merely means, "There is no benefit for us with David." See N. T. Wright, *Paul and the Faithfulness of God*, Christian Origins and the Question of God 4 (Minneapolis: Fortress, 2013), 2:825–36, esp. 829–30. Grant Macaskill, in a way similar to Wright, emphasizes the covenant with Israel and Christ as representative of Israel. See his *Union with Christ in the New Testament* (Oxford: Oxford University Press, 2013), esp. pp. 1–2, where he summarizes his position.

14. Or possibly "the faithfulness found in Christ Jesus" or "the faith relation experienced in Christ Jesus."

Mamshit baptistery

institution and 1 Corinthians 10:16: "Is not the cup of blessing which we bless a participation [*koinōnia*] in the blood [death] of Christ? Is not the bread which we break a participation [*koinōnia*] in the body of Christ?" Both the cup and the bread are a close engagement with Christ so that the significance of his life, death, and resurrection is remembered, brought forth in one's inner being, and mirrored in one's life.

The same thinking and more appears in 1 Corinthians 11:24–29. The words "This is my body for you" and "This cup is the new covenant in my blood" express Jesus's participation with humanity in giving his life and in establishing the new covenant by his death. Ingesting the bread and wine is an act of remembering Jesus, which surely means that people keep the significance of his death and life before their eyes, but it is also a participation, a joint sharing and identification, with his dying and rising.[15] Additionally, it is a proclamation of Jesus's death—and resurrection—until he comes. The act of ingesting requires discernment about the significance of Jesus's death and about one's life in relation to Jesus so that the ingesting is not a sham (vv. 27–28), as it was in the way the Corinthians were selfishly abusing the meal. Discerning the body is required (v. 29), but does that mean discerning the significance of Jesus's death, or discerning the significance of the church as the body of Christ—the subject of 1 Corinthians 12—or both? The primary focus is probably on discerning the significance of Jesus's death, but can one think of the significance of Jesus's death without thinking of the implications for the communal body of Christ? I think not. To remember Jesus's death is to be shaped by and to mirror his self-giving in the way one lives.

Baptism and the Lord's Supper are, then, the primary sources for participation thinking, and both are incorporative events, the one initiatory and the other a ritual act of remembering whereby the event is kept real. Neither baptism nor the Lord's Supper is merely a symbol, for much more is going on than that. Nor is either magic, as 1 Corinthians 10:1–11 is quick to point out with its analogy of the Israelites, who had a similar baptism "into Moses" and had food and drink provided by God but still failed, for their identity was not transformed. Instead, both baptism and the Lord's Supper are a means of being firmly anchored in Christ's identity so that he determines life. The early Christians knew that with their baptism they had abandoned one kind of life and had been taken up into another, that of the risen Lord. They also knew that with their frequent celebration of the Eucharist, they together were participating in the death, resurrection, and life of Christ and were bound to each other. No better

15. Hans Conzelmann says, "By this means the participant obtains a part in him, in the sacramental communion," and, "'Is' signifies . . . participation." *1 Corinthians: A Commentary on the First Epistle to the Corinthians*, Hermeneia (Philadelphia: Fortress, 1975), 198, 199.

explanation of participation exists than that found in baptism and the Lord's Supper.

The New Testament focus on participation is likewise evident in corporate images like body, temple, and new being. The temple and the new being can refer to the individual or to the community. These are important images, but the body is the fundamental metaphor in Paul's thought. We are *part of Christ* and *part of each other* because we are members of his body (see Rom. 12:5;[16] 1 Cor. 6:15; 12:27; Eph. 4:25; and 5:30).

In addition to the "in Christ" language, expressions of being "with" Christ and the prevalence of "with" compounds convey the same participation theology. Christians are crucified with Christ, raised with him, bound with him, engaged with him in his work, and similar ideas. This "with" language is important especially in Ephesians, which has fourteen occurrences of "with" or "with" compounds, and in Romans 6:4–8.[17] In fact, we could say Christian faith and life are understood via prepositions: we live in, with, to, by, and from the Lord. Any understanding of faith that does not include being joined with Christ is not Christian faith.

Is Participation Even Possible?

Does all this sound too strange, like something modern people cannot conceive or appropriate? Some think so. E. P. Sanders, who is largely responsible for the renewed focus on participation, after 521 pages of *Paul and Palestinian Judaism*, many showing

---

16. The NIV's "belongs to all the others" is unfortunate. The text says "are members of each other."

17. See such compounds and examples as *synklēronomos* ("heir with"), *syssōmos* ("body with"), *symmetochos* ("sharing with"—these first three all in Eph. 3:6), *symphytos* ("grown together" / "identified with," Rom. 6:5), *symmorphizein* ("taking the same form," Phil. 3:10), *symmorphos* ("formed with" / "conformed," Rom. 8:29), *sympolitēs* ("citizen with," Eph. 2:19), *sympaschein* ("suffer with," Rom. 8:17), *systauroun* ("crucify with," Rom. 6:6), *synegeirein* ("raise with," Eph. 2:6), *synergos* ("fellow worker," 1 Cor. 3:9), and numerous others.

how important the theme is in Paul's thought, on the last two pages says, "Righteousness by faith and participation in Christ ultimately amount to the same thing," and, "We lack a category of 'reality'—real participation in Christ," and then he stunningly adds, "To an appreciable degree, what Paul concretely thought cannot be directly appropriated by Christians today."[18] A lot of people must not have gotten the message!

Sanders was not the first to think this way. Johannes Weiss in the early twentieth century said, "It cannot be denied that Paul's Christology is inclined, upon one side, to abandon the firm lines laid down by concrete ideas of a definite personality." He thought Paul's ideas belonged to "an upper stratum of speculation" and resulted in "the sublimation and dissolution of personality."[19]

Are we so impoverished as Sanders and Weiss suggest? Modern identity theory does not view humans as individualistically as Weiss does. At issue is what it means to be human. Is one truly human when seen as an isolated and lone individual? Scripture and modern science say otherwise. Life is relational—both with God and with other people. Many of our problems exist because people assume human existence can be conceived of apart from God and then discuss how God and humans are joined. Scripture assumes that to be human is to be involved with God, willingly or not. Any proper understanding of a gospel of participation is grounded in a focus on God's participation with humans through Christ, as evidenced in the frequently repeated statement "He became what we are in order that we might become what he is."[20]

18. Sanders, *Paul and Palestinian Judaism*, 522–23.

19. Johannes Weiss, *Paul and Jesus*, trans. H. J. Chaytor (New York: Harper & Brothers, 1909), 22, 24.

20. This often-repeated statement is a modern summation of Irenaeus, *Against Heresies* 5, preface (cf. the quotations of Irenaeus on p. 27), and of Athanasius, *On the Incarnation of the Word* 54.3 ("For He was made man that we might be made God"), in *Nicene and Post-Nicene Fathers*, series 2, ed. Philip Schaff and Henry Wace (repr., Peabody, MA: Hendrickson, 1994), 4:65. God's participation with humans is assumed from creation on and especially with God's covenant with Israel.

As we will see, Paul was not the first to focus on participation ideas, and scholars regularly reject the narrow thinking of Sanders and Weiss. As one example, Susan Eastman argues we should think of a "participatory identity," for *fundamentally, humans are relationally constituted agents.* Human individuality presupposes relations, rather than the reverse. She argues, "Paul's anthropology is participatory all the way down," and she shows how such ideas can be used by moderns to understand ourselves and Christian living.[21]

None of us exists as an isolated entity. Context communicates life and relations. *Existence is always housed somewhere, and the idea of an isolated being without context and relations is an illusion.* Where and with whom is your identity housed? Your real context, if you are a Christian, is life in and with Christ, whatever other contexts you might inhabit. Your relation with God and all your relations with other people are housed in Christ and circumscribed by being in Christ.[22] This is largely what participation is about. Your identity and all your being are housed in Christ's identity. Geography is identity! Being in Christ assumes an "organic" relation with Christ, and this connection to Christ communicates life. Whereas the illusion of our culture is that life is our own private possession, the Scriptures always attest that life is not something we have independent of God. Two factors, then, are involved in what the New Testament writers understand with participation language: an understanding of identity and something organic, a sense of life being provided by and dependent on Christ.

Still, is not participation language too complicated for simple, ordinary people? Can they grasp participation? Of course they can, if they are the least reflective. People seem to have no difficulty grasping the idea of asking Christ into their hearts. Why, then, is

21. Susan Grove Eastman, *Paul and the Person: Reframing Paul's Anthropology* (Grand Rapids: Eerdmans, 2017), xii, 10, 15–16.

22. See, e.g., Philem. 8, 16, 20, 23.

participation in and with Christ more difficult to understand than asking Christ into one's heart? It is no easier to explain Christ in us than it is to explain our being in Christ!

People may feel more comfortable with the idea of Christ in us, for we then are the dominant personality, and Christ can be tucked away when convenient. Our being in Christ shifts that dominance away from our ego and gives real force to the confession "Jesus is Lord." Miroslav Volf correctly says, "Paul presumes a centered self, more precisely a *wrongly* centered self that needs to be de-centered by being nailed to the cross. . . . The self is never without a center; it is always engaged in the production of its own center."[23] Stated differently, Christian self-understanding is found outside the Christian; it is found in Christ. In dying with Christ and calling him Lord, we find a new and powerful center for the self.

Further, the biblical texts people love most are *texts that focus on participation*—texts such as Psalm 23 ("The Lord is *my* shepherd. . . . He leads *me*"), Matthew 28:20 ("I am with you always"), or Romans 8:38–39 (nothing will separate us from the love of God)—and people love these texts because of what they convey about God's presence with us and our involvement in life with God.

One of the biggest problems in the church, one pastors complain about repeatedly, is passivity. People, if they come, watch but do not engage. The Jewish scholar Abraham Heschel complained of people praying by proxy and never really praying themselves.[24] A huge difference exists between participating and watching. We have watchers, onlookers, an audience. People often do not engage in worship, in learning, or in productive living as Christians. One never has the impression from the New Testament, however, that Christians were or could be onlookers. Some may have been

---

23. Miroslav Volf, *Exclusion and Embrace* (Nashville: Abingdon, 1996), 69 (italics original).

24. Abraham Joshua Heschel, *Quest for God: Studies in Prayer and Symbolism* (New York: Crossroad, 1990), 49–51.

short on understanding, but they were not onlookers. They could not be, in those early days when faith placed them at odds with their world—but then authentic faith is always at odds with life that leaves God out of the picture. The worship of early Christians was participatory; they were expected to bring something to the service, like a psalm or a teaching (1 Cor. 14:26). Their lives were an engagement with Christ, as even letters addressing their problems attest.

How can the passivity of many Christians be changed? Perhaps we need to recover that sense of being at odds with the world. Passivity disappears the moment one takes participation with Christ's life, death, resurrection, and concerns seriously. You cannot participate with Christ and be passive.

What Advantage Comes from an Emphasis on Participation?

One of the first advantages of participation is that the confession "Jesus is Lord," one of the earliest confessions of the church, takes on a whole new meaning and significance. If one takes "in Christ" seriously, how could he not be Lord? Also, the faith/works discussion is virtually obliterated if participation categories are taken seriously. This discussion would not have been so prevalent if attention had been paid to such expressions as "work of faith" (1 Thess. 1:3), "faith working through love" (Gal. 5:6), or "the obedience of faith" (Rom. 1:5). Faith is something active, something we do. Faith works, or it is not faith. There are still questions about the impact of human sinfulness on participation and about how final judgment will assess Christian obedience, but one cannot think of participation with Christ that does not produce a Christlike character. How could one participate with Christ and not do his work?

Salvation thinking starts to make sense. Atonement theology presumes unity with Christ, or it is of no effect. Atonement is about identity with Christ in dying to sin, not theories of satisfaction, to take nothing away from discussions of the wrath of God, judgment, and the like.

Is there a difference between a person being in Christ and Christ being in a person? Yes! There is a difference in frequency, ethical impact, and ecclesiology. The idea of being in Christ is much more frequent in Scripture. Regarding the ethical impact, if we think of Christ in us, we are still the dominant person, but if we know we are in Christ, he is dominant and determines everything. Athanasius made the point that all things receive the characteristics of that in which they participate.[25] You cannot participate with Christ without being determined by him. Regarding ecclesiology, the idea of Christ being in a person lacks the corporate aspect that people being in Christ presupposes. Already in one of the earliest, if not *the* earliest, of Paul's Letters, he describes the Thessalonian Christians as imitators of *the churches of God in Judea in Christ Jesus* (1 Thess. 2:14). Again there is that profound double geography of living and serving in a geographical location and also being determined by being in Christ. *All the churches together are in Christ*, part of him and part of each other. Paul's body theology is a direct result of this thinking.

Not only is participation possible, it is what we were created for and what Christian faith is about. The following chapters will show that participation is the assumption of the Bible in all its parts, even though it is expressed in various ways. Participation is not just a theme from Paul and John. We will also explore what happens if we take the message seriously. Remember, though, that the topic is not just participation but the gospel, the good news, of participation. As we look at different parts of Scripture, by necessity we will deal with method in interpretation and with the fact that the gospel is presented in significantly different ways by the various writers.

25. Athanasius, *Orations against the Arians* 1.38–39; 3.23, 33–34. See Robert Letham, *Union with Christ in Scripture, History, and Theology* (Phillipsburg, NJ: P&R, 2011), 93.

The language in Scripture for participation ideas is also varied, and it is worth listing the primary words here. In the Old Testament, obviously "covenant" is a crucial idea, but so too are the Hebrew verbs *dābaq* ("cling" / "hold fast") and *lāvāh* ("join to"). In the New Testament, terms proliferate. In addition to *en Christō* and *en kyriō* ("in the Lord"), note *koinōnia* ("sharing"/"participation"), *koinōnos* ("partner"), *koinōnein* ("to share"), *menein* ("to remain"), *metochos* ("sharing"/"partner"), *metochē* ("sharing"), *syn* ("with"), and numerous *syn* compounds such as *systauroun* ("crucified with") and *symphytos* ("united").[26] We should mention as well *metousia* ("participation"), which is important in patristic literature.

26. See note 17 above.

four

Is the Gospel of Participation
in the Old Testament?

*Relationship with God is always and forever participation in the
preexisting* koinōnia *of the divine Persons. . . . I contend that to
be saved is to be renewed in the true image of God as women and
men in Christ, to have our relationality restored so that our sinful
selves, hopelessly* incurvatus in se, *are set free to be new creations
in true divine and human* koinōnia. . . . *Being saved, being in cov-
enantal relation, is God's first and only eternal plan of creation.*

Cherith Fee Nordling[1]

Not long ago a pastor wrote me to ask about a recent book arguing the Old Testament is obsolete, a house of cards, and not really
needed by Christians. That view is as old as Marcion in the second
century, but it is still heresy. The relation of the Old Testament
to the New Testament is a complex subject, but whatever else

---

1. Cherith Fee Nordling, "Being Saved as a New Creation: Co-humanity in the
True *Imago Dei*," in *What Does It Mean to Be Saved? Broadening Evangelical Horizons of Salvation*, ed. John G. Stackhouse Jr. (Grand Rapids: Baker Academic,
2002), 115–36, here 118, 122.

one says, the Old Testament is *absolutely foundational* for Jesus and the New Testament. If participation is not a theme in the Old Testament, then arguing for its importance will be an uphill battle. No worries! Participation is woven into the fabric of the Old Testament descriptions of God and his people. As Cherith Fee Nordling's statement above says, being in covenant relation is God's first and only eternal plan of creation and salvation.

But is the gospel in the Old Testament? Surely we want to answer this question affirmatively, but a lot depends on our definition of "gospel." What is the downside of seeing the gospel in the Old Testament, and what is the upside? The more our focus is on the death and resurrection of Jesus—and we surely do not want to diminish that focus—the less we may be inclined to see the gospel in the Old Testament. On the other hand, the life, death, and resurrection of Jesus do not exist as isolated events but are part of a larger narrative and assume the whole history of God's dealings with Israel and other nations. At issue is an understanding of the character of God by which the significance of the death and resurrection of Jesus may be understood. The early church worked out the theology of Jesus's death and resurrection by reading their *Old Testament* Scriptures. They had nothing else.

If there are six questions for understanding the gospel,[2] which of the six cannot be answered from the Old Testament?

1. Why does anyone need the gospel?
2. What is the gospel?
3. What, specifically, do the death and resurrection of Jesus have to do with the gospel?
4. To what degree is the gospel eschatological?
5. How is the gospel appropriated?
6. How should the gospel be articulated?

2. See p. 5.

Only the third cannot be answered from the Old Testament, but even there the Old Testament has precedents and anticipations, such as the theme of the rejection and exaltation of God's servant in Isaiah or of other righteous sufferers.

Still, the Old Testament is not one piece of cloth; it is highly divergent. Some of it is problematic and does not seem even to hint at the gospel. Christians have not been nearly nuanced enough in explaining the Old Testament. Not long ago the members of our church read through the Old Testament together. A friend came to me and said, "We have to talk; I am having trouble reading the Old Testament." My response was, "You should." A great deal of the Old Testament is not telling us how we should live. Much in the Old Testament seems contrary to the gospel, for there is enormous bloodshed, defeat of enemies, and anticipation of other nations serving Israel in its own land. This is not the picture in the New Testament, apart from some apocalyptic parts of Revelation that are bathed in imagery and were not intended to be—must not be—read literalistically.

The Old Testament presents a picture of one nation, Israel, that has a responsibility given by God, a responsibility often unfulfilled. The story of Israel is also a picture of human existence—sin, evil, pain, suffering, and all. Some of it is a horrible story, such as the abuse and murder of the concubine in Judges 19 or the tawdry story in 2 Samuel of David's sin with Bathsheba and its consequences. With much of the story, you are not supposed to go and do likewise! Further, not all of the Old Testament is quoted or alluded to in the New Testament. The New Testament *primarily* and most frequently uses Genesis, Exodus, Deuteronomy, Psalms, and Isaiah. Still, the whole of the Old Testament is Scripture, but not all in the same way, for the Old Testament documents differ in character and purpose. A narrative or a proverb is not a psalm, and we should not act as if they were.

We should not undervalue those parts of the Old Testament that seem offensive. They confront us and remind us of human sin, including our own. Further, as my Old Testament colleague Bob Hubbard advises me, they also remind us that there is always opposition to what God is doing. The Old Testament does not sugarcoat life; rather, it offers a realistic view of the fact that God too has enemies.

Things change with Jesus's coming and his death and resurrection. Something new has happened that rearranges everything. The sacrificial system is no longer the focus, even though texts about it still have things to teach us. The focus on the land of Israel and on political enemies drops out of the message of Jesus and the church, even while there is a refusal to let go of Israel. The option of violence is taken off the table. The promises of God's intervention to establish justice are being fulfilled, often in unexpected ways. The eschaton, the end time, has broken in and is present with Jesus and his kingdom, with his death and resurrection, and with the pouring out of the Spirit. These events solidify hope in the still-future fulfillment of God's ultimate promises for all creation. This "now and not yet" stance marks the whole of Christian existence. *A single hope encompasses both present living and the ultimate future.* The two cannot be divided. The Old Testament does not have this breaking in of the end time, but the tension between the present and future is there already (see Isa. 13; Joel 2–3; and Zeph. 1).

Without the Old Testament you cannot understand at all what is happening with Jesus. Repeatedly, the Old Testament points in various ways to the ultimate defeat of evil, surely the cry of every human heart. Sometimes it is expressed as God's coming to shepherd his people; sometimes as expectations of a coming righteous king, "the Root of Jesse" or "the Branch," who would rule in righteousness; and sometimes as the expectation of the pouring out of God's Spirit to transform lives (Ezek. 36:25–26). The promises to Israel are seen as fulfilled in Jesus's work, in the movement of the Spirit in early Christianity, and in the way early Christians borrowed descriptions of Israel as their own self-designations. The

Old Testament is part of the gospel message at the same time as parts of the Old Testament are transcended, but it has a vision of what should be in God's world—God's kingdom.

Further, much of the Old Testament is a revelation of the character of God and what God desires of his people, and again, without the Old Testament you could not begin to understand what happened with Jesus. The Old Testament also tells of people who understood what God desired and who lived their faith at great cost and, especially with the Psalms and the Prophets, knew how to worship, lament, and confront their contemporaries, often with brutal honesty and moving expressions of their own emotions. The long and short of all this is that the church needs to be much more skilled in reading the Old Testament and recognizing the *function* of specific texts and their variegated nature.

Does the Old Testament Have a Gospel, and Does It Speak of Participation?

Major themes of the New Testament gospel are anchored in numerous Old Testament texts: the vindication of God (God will be shown to be in the right); the revelation of God and God's intent; the vision of what creation is supposed to be and of life lived with God, life as participation with God. The gospel tells of a just God who is *for us* because of grace, love, and covenant loyalty, a God who is with us, who transforms us, and who will defeat evil. That is the good news every human needs, and it is the message of the Old Testament.

That God is *for us* is Paul's assumption in Romans 8:31, part of his summary of the gospel, but it is already the assumption of the Old Testament in Psalm 56:9 (Hebrew v. 10): "This I know, that God is *for me*" (*'elohim li*); 118:6–7: "Yahweh is for me" (*yahveh li*); and 124:1: "If Yahweh had not been for us" (*lule yahveh she-hayah lanu*). Some translations render the last two as "the Lord with me" or "the Lord on our side," which is fine, but the text merely has the preposition *le* ("to," "for," "in regard to").[3] God is for us, which is the foundation of the gospel.

The Old Testament is filled with good news about this God who is for us, good news based in the character of God, and often this is expressed in ways quite similar to the New Testament. The wise woman of Tekoa describes God as one *who devises ways to bring back the banished* (2 Sam. 14:14), a description not unlike Jesus's parable of the prodigal son. Psalm 36:5–9 emphasizes the love and care of God:

> Your love, LORD, reaches to the heavens,
>   your faithfulness to the skies.
> Your righteousness is like the highest mountains,
>   your justice like the great deep.
>   You, LORD, preserve both people and animals.
> How priceless is your unfailing love, O God!
>   People take refuge in the shadow of your wings.
> They feast on the abundance of your house;
>   you give them drink from your river of delights.
> For with you is the fountain of life;
>   in your light we see light. (NIV)

Psalm 103, which a German scholar suggests was Jesus's favorite psalm,[4] expresses the gospel as strongly as any text. The Lord is the one

> who forgives all your sins
>   and heals all your diseases,
> who redeems your life from the pit
>   and crowns you with love and compassion. . . .

3. Other texts express the same idea, such as Num. 23:21; Deut. 32:9; Pss. 46:2–8; and 91:15.

4. Otto Betz, "Jesu Lieblingspsalm: Die Bedeutung von Psalm 103 für das Werk Jesu," *Theologische Beiträge* 15 (1984): 253–69.

The LORD works righteousness
    and justice for all the oppressed. . . .

The LORD is compassionate and gracious,
    slow to anger, abounding in love.
He will not always accuse,
    nor will he harbor his anger forever;
he does not treat us as our sins deserve
    or repay us according to our iniquities.
For as high as the heavens are above the earth,
    so great is his love for those who fear him;[5]
as far as the east is from the west,
    so far has he removed our transgressions from us.

As a father has compassion on his children,
    so the LORD has compassion on those who fear him.
        (103:3–4, 6, 8–13 NIV)

Foundational for any discussion of the gospel is the story of Abraham in Genesis, for it concerns the promise to Abraham that God would create a nation that would lead to blessing *for the whole world* (Gen. 12:3). The purpose of God's mission is not limited to Israel. The subsequent narrative emphasizes trust in God (esp. 15:6) and God's involvement in the lives of people. For example, Hagar tells of seeing the God who sees her (16:13), and God promises to be with Isaac and Jacob (26:24 and 28:15; see also 49:24–26). The main point is that God establishes a covenant with Abraham and his descendants (15:18; 17:1–8), promising to be with them and bless them but also binding them to himself and to his commands. This covenant relation involves participation by necessity.

The exodus narrative is equally foundational for the gospel and the New Testament. Freedom, which Paul views as the summary

5. Do remember that in the Old Testament, love for God and fear of God are parallels (see Deut. 10:12). This hardly fits our concept of fear. In Ps. 115:11 those who fear the Lord are those who trust him.

of the gospel (Gal. 5:1), is the focus with the exodus, but it is freedom *to be in the covenant*—the promise relation—which God establishes with his people. Exodus 6:6–7 sets the agenda as God tells Moses, "Therefore, say to the Israelites: 'I am the LORD, and I will bring you out from under the yoke of the Egyptians. I will free you from being slaves to them, and I will redeem you with an outstretched arm and with mighty acts of judgment. *I will take you as my own people, and I will be your God.* Then you will know that I am the LORD your God, who brought you out from under the yoke of the Egyptians" (NIV; italics mine). Much of the rest of Exodus focuses on the covenant God establishes and the obligations, such as the Ten Commandments, it brings. The Ten Commandments are the requirements of living in the covenant, the *instructions* showing people how they are to live in covenant relation to God. In Exodus 19:3–8 the people affirm they will do all God has said—that they will keep the covenant with God—even before the Ten Commandments are given in 20:2–17. Then, in 24:1–11, the covenant is formally established by sacrifice, and the people again affirm that they will obey God in everything (v. 7).

But why is there all this focus on God making a covenant, this tremendously important arrangement involving both a promise of relation and obligations for both God and his people? It is because of the words "I will take you as my own people, and I will be your God." This language is frequent: Leviticus 26:12; Deuteronomy 29:13; 2 Samuel 7:24; Jeremiah 7:23; 11:4; 30:22; 31:31–34; Ezekiel 36:28; see also 2 Corinthians 6:18. The covenant is about God and people living together. There are a variety of other texts stressing that God has chosen his people, loves them, and will be with them. *The first reality about the gospel is that God is for us and intends to have a people.* Everything else flows from that. God is not, then, some distant deity, but a God who seeks people to live in relation with him, *participating* in the life he gives. We must not forget that the word "testament," as in Old Testament and New

Testament, is a word for "covenant." The two parts of Scripture are about the older covenants God established with Israel and the new covenant established through Jesus Christ.

This privilege of being bound to God in covenant, however, is not merely about privilege. Election always implies responsibility, responsibility for the purposes of God, and being in covenant with God means being involved in the mission of God. The covenant with Abraham was for the blessing of all people (Gen. 12:3), and this theme resurfaces in various texts and images. The covenant people are to be a light to the nations (Isa. 49:6), all people are called to worship God, and the promise is that one day all people will do so (see texts like Isa. 2:2–4).

The exodus narrative underscores this participation of and with God in the description of the cloud by day and a fire by night and of the tabernacle, all three symbolizing the presence of God in the middle of the people. Later, the temple in Jerusalem does the same thing. God lives with his people, is engaged with their lives, and participates with them.

In many ways the gospel *must* be defined in terms of covenant. The promise of Jeremiah 31:31–34 is that God will make a new covenant in the future:

> "The days are coming," declares the LORD,
>   "when I will make a new covenant
> with the people of Israel
>   and with the people of Judah.
> It will not be like the covenant
>   I made with their ancestors
> when I took them by the hand
>   to lead them out of Egypt,
> because they broke my covenant,
>   though I was a husband to them,"
>   declares the LORD.
> "This is the covenant I will make with the people of Israel
>   after that time," declares the LORD.

"I will put my law in their minds
    and write it on their hearts.[6]
I will be their God,
    and they will be my people.
No longer will they teach their neighbor,
    or say to one another, 'Know the LORD,'
because they will all know me,
    from the least of them to the greatest,"
        declares the LORD.
"For I will forgive their wickedness
    and will remember their sins no more." (NIV)

Jesus and the early church saw this new covenant being fulfilled in what took place with the gospel events of the cross and the resurrection, as shown most obviously in the words of the Lord's Supper (Matt. 26:26–29/Mark 14:22–25/Luke 22:18–20/1 Cor. 11:23–25) and in 2 Corinthians 3 and Hebrews 8–10.

The Gospel in Isaiah

Dozens of other Old Testament texts could be listed that are potent expressions of the gospel, but surely Isaiah takes pride of place in announcing the gospel and deserves attention. With the verb *basar* ("to bring news, esp. good news") Isaiah emphasizes that he has good news. In 40:9 we find, "You who *bring good news* to Zion, go up on a high mountain. You who *bring good news* to Jerusalem, lift up your voice with a shout, lift it up, do not be afraid; say to the towns of Judah, 'Here is your God!'" (NIV).[7] Isaiah 52:7 has

6. On God writing his laws in people's hearts, see Ezek. 36:25–28 and Joel 2:28–32 (Hebrew 3:1–5).

7. The NIV rendering is preferable to the NRSV. The latter views Zion and Jerusalem as the heralds instead of the recipients of the news ("Get you up to a high mountain, O Zion, herald of good tidings; lift up your voice with strength, O Jerusalem, herald of good tidings, lift it up, do not fear; say to the cities of Judah, 'Here is your God!'"). See 41:27. The participles for the one announcing the good news are *feminine*.

the familiar words: "How beautiful upon the mountains are the feet of *the one who brings good news*, who proclaims peace, who *brings news of* good things, who proclaims salvation, who says to Zion, 'Your God reigns.'" (Paul quotes part of this verse in Rom. 10:15 and alludes to it in Eph. 2:17.) Then Isaiah 61:1–2a is even more detailed: "The Spirit of the Lord, Yahweh, is on me, because Yahweh anointed me to *bring good news* to the poor. He sent me to bind up the brokenhearted, to proclaim freedom for the captives and release for the prisoners, to proclaim the year of Yahweh's favor." Jesus, of course, found these words formative for his own self-understanding and mission, as his quotation of verses 1–2a in Luke 4:18–19 shows.[8] We will treat this text a bit later.[9]

In addition to its use of *basar* to express the telling of the good news, the content of Isaiah includes some of the most cherished and expressive gospel words of hope in Scripture. The following summaries provide a sample; notice how often there is focus on God's *Spirit*:

1. In the last days the mountain of the Lord's temple will be exalted, and all nations will stream to it to learn from the Lord. People will beat swords into plowshares, and there will be no more war or learning about war (Isa. 2:2–5; also in Mic. 4:1–4).

2. People walking in darkness have seen a great light; they rejoice before the Lord; the yoke of the oppressor has been shattered. For to us a child is born, and the government will be on his shoulders. He will be called Wonderful Counselor, Mighty God, Everlasting Father, Prince of Peace, and of the greatness of his government and peace there will be no end. He will reign with justice and righteousness forever (Isa. 9:2–7).

8. The form of the quotation in Luke also has words from Isa. 35:5 and 42:7. Isaiah 61 also stands behind the first two Beatitudes in Matt. 5:3–4. See also the uses of *basar* in Nah. 1:15 (Hebrew 2:1) and Ps. 68:11.

9. See pp. 83–87.

3. A shoot will come up from the stump of Jesse, a Davidic Branch will bear fruit, and the *Spirit* of the Lord will rest on him, the *Spirit* of wisdom, understanding, counsel, might, knowledge, and fear of the Lord. He will judge with righteousness on behalf of the poor, and he will punish the wicked. (Part of the good news is that God will judge evil. The vindication *of God* is at stake.) The wolf will live with the lamb, and there will not be harm or destruction, for the earth will be filled with the knowledge of the Lord as the waters cover the sea. Nations will rally to this Root of Jesse (Isa. 11:1–10).

4. The Lord will prepare *a celebration banquet for all people and will destroy death*. He will wipe away tears and disgrace and will save his people (Isa. 25:6–9).

5. Within a passionate prayer of trust in the Lord and conviction that right will prevail (Isa. 26) comes one of the earliest expectations of *resurrection*: "Your dead will live; their bodies will rise. . . . Wake up and shout with joy because your dew is radiant dew, and the earth will give birth to the dead" (Isa. 26:19; see also Dan. 12:2).

6. God comes to comfort his people and to rule with power. God's glory is revealed. Like a shepherd tending his flock, he carries the lambs and gently leads those that have young (Isa. 40:1–11).

7. God's servant will have God's *Spirit* on him, and he will bring justice to the nations. God will take his hand and make him a covenant for the people and a light for the gentiles, to open eyes that are blind, to free captives from prison, and to release from the dungeon those who sit in darkness. The Lord will triumph over his enemies (Isa. 42:1–16).

8. People will know the Lord and that he reigns. There is great joy at this gospel message. The Lord has comforted and redeemed his people, and all the earth will see the salvation of God (Isa. 52:6–10).

9. The servant is pierced and crushed for the sins of others. God's righteous servant will justify many and bear their iniquities, but he will be vindicated by God (Isa. 53:1–11).

10. The Lord has looked and seen there is no truth or justice and is appalled that there is no one to intervene. So, God puts on righteousness and salvation as if they are armor and comes to judge people according to what they have done. People everywhere will fear the Lord and revere him. The Redeemer will come to Zion and make a covenant with those who repent, and this covenant promises that God's *Spirit* will always be with them and his word on their lips forever (Isa. 59:12–21).

11. The *Spirit* of the Lord is on his servant to proclaim to the poor good news of freedom, comfort, healing, setting things right (which involves both retribution and reward), and an everlasting covenant. All the people will be called priests of the Lord (Isa. 61:1–11).

Numerous other texts from Isaiah and from other books could be presented that focus on the love and care of God and on God coming to redeem his people, but everywhere in the Old Testament that the good news is expressed or anticipated, there is a focus on God's *participation* with people and their *participation* with him. Participation is the nature of covenant, for covenants come with promises from both sides and obligations for both—especially if the focus is on the promise of God to be their God and of people to be his people. All that focus on the faithfulness/lovingkindness (*hesed*) of God is to show that God keeps his covenant with his people[10] and that obedience to the commands is the way people

10. The foundational text for these ideas is Exod. 34:4–7, a crucial text about the revelation of God's character that influenced numerous Old Testament texts, such as Neh. 9:17–19, 27–31; Pss. 86:5–16; 103:8; 145:8; Joel 2:13; and Jon. 4:2. New Testament writers also adapt Exod. 34:4–7 and its larger context to describe Jesus. See pp. 91–92, 99–100.

keep their covenant with God. Participation is the lens from which the Old Testament should be understood.

Often, we see the failure of people to participate. The recognition of this failure comes in the form of complaints that people do rituals but do not serve God; they go through the motions, but they do not participate. This is the complaint of both psalmists and prophets. See, for example, Psalm 50; Isaiah 1 and 66; Jeremiah 7 (esp. v. 23); Micah 6; and numerous other passages. Texts like these show that humans are religious beings but not righteous beings. We use religion as a mask or a covering, but we do not live in the close relation to God for which we were created.

Faith and Attachment in the Old Testament

The Old Testament language used to express faith as a close relation to God—a participation with God—has been neglected in the church, but one particular idea deserves special attention: that of being attached to or clinging to God. In chapter 2 we saw that Martin Luther talked about faith as being cemented to Christ. He was not the first to use such language of attachment. The Hebrew word *dabaq* is used of attachment and holding fast to something or someone, and it expresses what faith is about. It is used generally of people in dire straits whose skin *clings* to their bones, as in Job 19:20, or their soul to the dust, as in Psalm 119:25.[11] It is used of the tongue clinging to the roof of the mouth in speechlessness, as in Ezekiel 3:26, or in desperate hunger, as in Lamentations 4:4. It is used of a husband clinging to his wife, as in Genesis 2:24,[12] or of Ruth clinging to Naomi or to the workers of Boaz (Ruth 1:14; and 2:8, 21, 23). It is used of clinging to the decrees of God (Ps. 119:31), but of the sixty occurrences of the word, *most significantly, ten of them are used of clinging to*

---

11. See also Ps. 102:5.

12. See also Gen. 34:3, of Shechem's soul being attached to Dinah, and 2 Kings 11:2, of Solomon clinging to foreign wives.

or holding fast to the Lord. Five of the ten are in Deuteronomy and are formulaic summaries of what faith in God really is. For example, 13:4 (Hebrew v. 5) says, "You will follow the Lord your God, you will fear him, you will keep his commandments, you will obey his voice, you will serve him, and you will *cling to him*," and 30:19–20 says, "Today I call the heavens and the earth as witnesses against you that I have placed before you life and death, blessing and curse. Choose life so that you and your children may live and that you may love the Lord your God, obey his voice, and *cling to him*, because he is your life."[13] Joshua 22:5; 23:8; 2 Kings 18:6 (of Hezekiah); Psalm 63:8 (Hebrew v. 9); and Jeremiah 13:11 all have this same emphasis on *clinging or holding fast* to God.[14] If people today knew and took seriously that faith meant clinging to God, their lives would change.

But this is not the only Hebrew word that conveys the idea of being bound to God. *Lavah* does as well. This word, too, is used of being attached or bound to a spouse (Gen. 29:34) or family/group (Num. 18:2),[15] but most importantly, it is also used of being bound or joined to the Lord. Isaiah 56:3 says, "Do not let the foreigner who has *joined himself to* the Lord say, 'The Lord will surely separate me from his people.'" Similarly, Zechariah 2:10–11 (Hebrew vv. 14–15) promises that God will come and live among his people and that "many nations will *be joined to* the Lord in that day and will become my people." See also Isaiah 56:6 ("And foreigners who *join themselves to* the Lord to minister to him, to love the name of the Lord, and to be his servants . . .") and Jeremiah 50:5 ("They will come and *join themselves to* the Lord with an everlasting covenant that will not be forgotten").

13. See also Deut. 4:4; 10:20; and 11:22.

14. My colleague Jim Bruckner says "clinging" as an ultimate act of faith is illustrated without equal in Hab. 3:16–19, even though the word is not specifically in the text. In this text, everything has gone wrong, and the situation is terrible, but Habakkuk says, "Yet I will exult/triumph in the Lord; I will rejoice in God my Savior" (v. 18), which sounds very much like Paul's "Rejoice in the Lord" (Phil. 3:1).

15. See also Num. 18:4; Esther 9:27; Ps. 83:8 (Hebrew v. 9); and Isa. 14:1.

The gospel says God will live with his people, and it views faith as being joined to, bound to, this God. Participation is the assumption throughout.

It is no surprise, then, that the Jewish scholar Abraham Heschel says, "Faith is attachment. . . . Faith is an act of the whole person, of mind, will, and heart. Faith is sensitivity, understanding, engagement, and attachment, not something achieved once and for all, but an attitude one may gain and lose."[16] Faith is a lived attachment to God.

Other texts express this intimate participation with God via images of family, especially marriage. Often, God is viewed as the husband of his people, and nowhere is this expressed more powerfully than in Hosea 1–3. See also, among others, Isaiah 54:5; Jeremiah 3:14, 20; and 31:32. Elsewhere, Israel is called God's son (Exod. 4:22 and Hosea 11:1), and people are viewed as God's children (Deut. 14:1; Isa. 63:16; and Jer. 31:1–3, 9).

Surprisingly, given Christian language, the Old Testament has little focus on the noun "faith." The NIV uses "faith" in the Old Testament only ten times, and only four of those refer to faith in God. The NRSV has only eighteen, six referring to faith in God. The Hebrew word for faith, *'emunah*, however, occurs forty-nine times, twenty-two of which refer to the *faithfulness of God*. One such example is in the statement (and the song) everyone loves, "Great is thy faithfulness," which is from Lamentations 3:23 and describes God's *'emunah*, his faithfulness even in the bleakest of times. The word *'emunah* is more about reliability, constancy, and truth than thinking. It derives from the verb *'aman*, which has a range of connotations: "to be firm, reliable, trustworthy, enduring" and "to believe in, trust in."[17] The Hebrew word for

---

16. Abraham Joshua Heschel, *God in Search of Man: A Philosophy of Judaism* (New York: Farrar, Straus & Giroux, 1955), 154.

17. "Believe in" is primarily in the *hiphil* verb form. See R. W. L. Moberly, "אמן," *New International Dictionary of Old Testament Theology & Exegesis*, ed. W. VanGemeren (Grand Rapids: Zondervan, 1997), 1:430–31. Moberly says *'emunah* conveys the attractiveness of moral living.

"truth" (*'emet*) is from the same verb. These words are all covenant words. One who has *'emunah*—faith/faithfulness—keeps a covenant. One of the most important occurrences of the verb is in Genesis 15:6, which tells of Abraham trusting God and his trust being credited as righteousness—keeping the covenant.

Pistis, the Greek word for "faith" that is so important in the New Testament, occurs only thirty-three times in the Greek translation of the Old Testament, thirteen of those in the historical part of the canon, eight in Jeremiah, and seven in Proverbs.[18] *Pistis* is not used of the content of believing or of the fact that one believes. It is used of faithfulness and honesty. *Pistis* is what one does, as we saw earlier. For example, Proverbs 12:22 says, "Lying lips are an abomination to the Lord, but the one doing faithfulness [*poiōn pisteis*] is acceptable to him."

A crucial and revealing use of *'emunah* and of *pistis* is, of course, Habakkuk 2:4, but should it be translated as it is in the NRSV ("the righteous live by *their* faith"), or as it is in the NIV ("the righteous person will live by *his* faithfulness")? The Hebrew has only the equivalent of "the righteous will live by *his* faith/faithfulness," but whose faith/faithfulness? God's, or that of the righteous person? The Greek in Paul's quotations of this verse in Romans 1:17 and Galatians 3:11 also could be taken either way,[19] but the Septuagint, the Greek translation of the Old Testament, makes a decision and adds the word *mou* ("my") to explain that the reference is to God's faithfulness: "The righteous will live by *my* faithfulness." I am fairly confident that the Septuagint is correct and that the focus in both Hebrew and Greek is on *God's* faithfulness, but in the end it may not matter, for there is always a

18. Plus one each in Deuteronomy, Hosea, Habakkuk, Psalms, and Song of Songs. There are twenty-five occurrences of *pistis* in the Old Testament Apocrypha, and the same focus on faithfulness, honesty, and similar ideas dominates. Even in 4 Macc. 15:24; 16:22; and 17:2, which tell of the faith of a mother whose seven sons are martyred, the focus is on what her faith does, not on its content.

19. Paul does not include the pronoun in either Rom. 1:17 or Gal. 3:11. Hebrews 10:38 has "My righteous one will live by faith."

double-sidedness to "faith/faithfulness."[20] Faith always is directed at something faithful, something meriting trust. "To say 'I have faith' is to say nothing about myself, but to say that God is a trustworthy God."[21] If both the Greek and Hebrew words translated "faith" equally carry the connotation of "faithfulness," which they most certainly do, can a person have faith without being faithful? Such a thought would seem foolish to the biblical writers. Having faith means being bound into a faithful relation with God and living it out. In other words, it means participation.

Do not get the idea, though, that faith is an unimportant theme in the Old Testament. Other words, such as "trust" (*batah*) and "hope" (*qavah*), are frequent, but perhaps, since "faith" is now understood so anemically, we should focus more on words like "trust," "loyalty," "cling," or "adhere to." Such language would do justice to the ideas of participation that dominate Scripture.

Other texts and images have the same understanding. One of the most powerful metaphors in Scripture is the idea of walking with God. Leviticus 26:12, for example, says, "And I will walk among you, and will be your God, and you shall be my people" (NRSV), and Psalm 26:3 says, "For your steadfast love is before my eyes, and I will walk in your faithfulness." "Walk" is a frequent metaphor in both Testaments for life with God, although translations sometimes erase the metaphor by using "live." Further, these two texts and numerous others describing life as a walk with God do not use the simple *qal* form of the Hebrew verb for "walk," *halak*. They use the *hithpael*, which carries the connotation of "walking about" and is used both of God walking about with his people and of Enoch, Noah, Abraham, Hezekiah, and the psalm-

---

20. Romans 1:17 says, "The righteousness of God is being revealed from faith to faith [*ek pisteōs eis pistin*]." How that should be understood is debated, but a good case can be made that the intent is "from God's faithfulness leading to human faithfulness." See N. T. Wright, *Paul and the Faithfulness of God*, Christian Origins and the Question of God 4 (Minneapolis: Fortress, 2013), 2:1466–71.

21. D. H. van Daalen, "Faith according to Paul," *Expository Times* 87 (1975): 83–85, esp. 84.

ists walking about with God.[22] When people understand that faith means a life of walking around with God, then everything changes, and participation ideas receive their justice.

Other poignant images of participation with God appear in the Old Testament. In Psalm 73:23, after wrestling with the problem of evil and complaining of his own stupidity, the psalmist says to God, "Yet I am always with you; you grasp me by my right hand." The rest of the psalm underscores God's leading and blessing, how central God is to the psalmist's life, how good it is to be near God, and how much God is his refuge. Participation is also implied with the command to tie the law between one's eyes and on one's arms (Deut. 6:8). This was a graphic way to underscore that the relation with God was to dominate all that people saw and did.

There is one remaining feature in the Old Testament that we need to examine: we would not expect the Old Testament to have anything equivalent to being in Christ, but it does. Psalm 90:1 is most remarkable: "Lord, you have been our dwelling place throughout all generations." The same idea is in Psalms 71:3 and 91:9 and in those texts that view God as a fortress or a rock of refuge for the righteous (e.g., Pss. 18:2; 28:8; 31:2–3; 46:1–11; and Jer. 16:9). The idea of living with God is also present in texts such as Psalm 61:4 (Hebrew v. 5): "Let me dwell in your tent forever and take refuge in the shelter of your wings."

One of the questions that continually surfaces is the relation of divine initiative and human response. How much depends on God, and how much on us? We will encounter the question again later, but Scripture rarely—if ever—sees this as a problem the way modern theologians do or views the two as antithetical. Some, at least, in ancient Israel seemed to know God was already at work in their response. For example, Joel 2:32 (Hebrew 3:5) has a double calling: "Everyone who *calls* on the name of the Lord will be delivered . . . even among the survivors whom the *Lord calls*."

22. See, e.g., Gen. 5:24; 6:9; 17:1; 2 Kings 20:3; Pss. 26:3; 56:13 (Hebrew v. 14); and 116:9.

Jeremiah 31:18 says, "Turn me, and I will turn."[23] Further, God is always the one who acts first in establishing a covenant; God never merely responds to human initiatives. This is part of the good news. God is indeed for us.

From the evidence in this chapter, no doubt can exist whether there is good news—gospel—in the Old Testament, and no doubt can exist that faith is about participation with God. God chooses to participate in the lives of his people and dwells in their midst, and God expects them to be bound to him, to cling to him, to walk with him, and to participate in life with him.

People cannot be bound to God without having their identity reshaped by God's character, without having the concerns God has, and without being engaged in the work God is doing. Old Testament writers knew that both God's credibility and Israel's own credibility were at stake in the way people kept the covenant. That is still the case with the gospel. The credibility of the gospel depends, to some degree, at least, on the willingness of its adherents to mirror the character of their God. Why have a God who does not change the way you live? We can only ask what difference it would make in the lives of modern Christians if they took seriously that faith is being bound to God and participating with God. Could people still fail to have a living faith?

---

23. Also Lam. 5:21.

five

The Gospels in the Synoptic Gospels

We understand Christ only if we commit ourselves to him in a stark "Either-Or." He did not go to the cross to ornament and embellish our life. If we wish to have him, then he demands the right to say something decisive about our entire life. We do not understand him if we arrange for him only a small compartment in our spiritual life. . . . The religion of Christ is not a tidbit after one's bread; on the contrary, it is bread or it is nothing.

Dietrich Bonhoeffer[1]

The title of this chapter underscores that the Gospels present both the gospel Jesus preached *and to some extent* the gospel of the Gospel writers. These two messages are closely related, but they are not the same. They could not be, because of the shift in gravity caused by Jesus's death and vindication/resurrection. These events were anticipated by Jesus but were not the focus of his message. In addition, each Gospel writer nuances his understanding of the gospel differently than the other writers do.

1. Dietrich Bonhoeffer, "Jesus Christ and the Essence of Christianity," trans. Geffrey B. Kelly, in *A Testament to Freedom: The Essential Writings of Dietrich Bonhoeffer*, ed. Geffrey B. Kelly and F. Burton Nelson (San Francisco: HarperCollins, 1990), 51.

The surprising fact is that the message of the evangelists and the early church was *not* merely read back onto the lips of Jesus. Subjects the church cared about—such as circumcision, the admission of gentiles, the apostolic office, or the continuing place of Israel—are either not mentioned or rarely treated by Jesus. Conversely, the main subjects during Jesus's ministry—such as Sabbath keeping, ritual purity, parables, and to some extent the kingdom of God—recede or are rarely mentioned in the church's message, and the parables are not referred to at all. Even the Christology of the Gospels is not that of the early church. "Son of Man" is the most frequent self-designation of Jesus, and he deflects the term "Christ" ("the Anointed One," "the Messiah"), even as he fulfills the messianic promises. With the church, "Son of Man" hardly appears, and "Christ" and "Lord" become the main titles. Further, the Gospels, especially the Synoptics, have relatively little explanation of the significance of Jesus's death. When the narrative comes to the crucifixion scene, the Gospels say nothing more than "They crucified him." The evangelists seem content merely to tell the story. No modern Christian would write a Gospel this way.

The evangelists are not bashful about laying out their own views of who Jesus is. The beginning of each Gospel reveals clearly how each evangelist understands the significance of Jesus, even before they get into the story. Early in their accounts all four emphasize the fulfillment of the Old Testament promises, use Isaiah 40:3 (which speaks of preparing the way of the Lord), affirm that Jesus is the Son of God, and emphasize that he is anointed with the Spirit. In all four, Jesus as king is a central theme that finds its climax with the crucifixion and the inscription above the cross, "The King of the Jews."

The first verse in Matthew underscores that the story is about the promised covenants with David and Abraham, and by 1:21–23 the reader knows that Jesus will save his people from sins and that "they will call his name 'Immanuel,'" "God with us"—which does not literally happen in the story but is a way of underscoring that

Jesus is the very presence of God with humans. In 2:1–2 the reader knows Jesus is the king of the Jews.

Mark is least explicit, but his first verse, too, already labels Jesus as the Messiah and Son of God, although the latter may be an addition. It is missing in a few manuscripts.

Luke's introduction is much longer, but early on, the reader is told that Mary's child will reign forever (1:32–33); that he is the Savior and the Messiah (1:69; 2:11), and that he brings revelation to the gentiles and glory for Israel (2:26–32). In the next chapter we will see that the prologue of John is even more forceful in its description.

The convictions of the evangelists are quite clear, but especially for the Synoptics, those convictions are more the backdrop of the story or its presuppositions, and the story itself unfolds in much more muted fashion with those presuppositions needing to be proven. Even in John the distinction between the ministry of Jesus and the time after the resurrection is clearly and frequently marked (e.g., 2:22).

The Four Essential Ingredients of *Jesus's* Gospel

To ignore the gospel Jesus preached—the gospel *of* Jesus—or to collapse it into the gospel *about* Jesus lessens Jesus's Jewishness and his focus on Israel and diminishes crucial themes. The gospel Jesus preaches in the Synoptics is centered on compassion, celebration, Israel, and the kingdom of heaven/God.[2] The kingdom is the foundation of the first three features, and all four have deep ethical implications.

Compassion. Compassion—deep sensitivity and love—dominates the message and activities of Jesus. The good news is about the compassion of God revealed and demonstrated by Jesus. Compassion

2. See Klyne Snodgrass, "The Gospel of Jesus," in *The Written Gospel*, ed. Markus Bockmuehl and Donald A. Hagner (Cambridge: Cambridge University Press, 2005), 31–44.

motivates his healings and his feeding of the multitudes (Matt. 9:36 and 15:32). He assures us that our Father cares for birds and that we are worth much more than they (Matt. 6:26). This is only a way to say what we have already seen: *God is for us.* Jesus focuses on forgiveness and on the Father's knowing our needs and being eager to respond to them. Jesus urges those who are toiling and burdened to come to him, saying he will give them rest. He urges them to take his yoke—join in his work, participate in what he is doing—and learn from him (Matt. 11:28–29). Jesus does not allow limits for compassion, as his command to love one's enemies shows.[3] The focus on compassion is present in all four Gospels and is itself a fulfillment of Old Testament expectations of God coming to show redemptive compassion (e.g., Isa. 40:10–11; 49:13–22; 57:15–19; Joel 2:13–32; and Zech. 10:6).

Do not take the love and compassion of God for granted. Today, people—if they believe in God at all—just assume God is compassionate and loving, but where did they get that idea? That God is love is *specifically* Christian teaching. Religions prior to Christianity and ones not based on Christianity do not generally see the gods or god as loving. Larry Hurtado, in his significant book *Destroyer of the Gods*, says that people in the Greco-Roman period had a sense of religious awe and even a particular affection for their favorite deities and that there are references to this or that pagan deity being merciful or generous. "But the notion that the gods love humanity with anything approaching relational intensity ascribed to God rather ubiquitously in early Christian texts is, to put it mildly, hard to find in pagan texts of the Greek or Roman period. . . . We simply do not know of any other Roman era religious group in which love played this important role in the discourse or behavioral teaching."[4] Even in the Old Testament, in which God is said to love Israel, only by implication is

---

3. See Matt. 5:44; see also 18:22.
4. Larry W. Hurtado, *Destroyer of the Gods: Early Christian Distinctiveness in the Roman World* (Waco: Baylor University Press, 2016), 65.

there evidence of God's love for all people. But God's love and compassion even for enemies is at the heart of the good news of Jesus and the New Testament.

Celebration. Celebration is also a necessary component in describing Jesus's message, a message he himself explains with good-news (*euangelion*) language (e.g., Matt. 11:5 and Mark 8:35). If people grasped the significance of his coming, they would be dancing in the streets (Luke 7:31–34). They would be like a person who found a treasure in a field and, from joy, sold everything to purchase the field (Matt. 13:44–45). Jesus's meals with sinners are clear anticipations of the messianic banquet of Isaiah 25:6–10 and allow people to participate in such celebration now and find forgiveness. With parables like the banquet (Luke 14:15–24) and the prodigal and elder son (Luke 15:11–32), Jesus, in effect, is saying, "God is giving a party. Are you going to come?" The lost are being found, and it is *necessary* to celebrate their return. Fasting is not appropriate, for the time of Jesus is a time of celebration (Matt. 9:15/Mark 2:19/Luke 5:34).

The Beatitudes and other "blessed" sayings are calls to celebrate, but they are not general calls to be happy. In most cases they point to celebration that God's long-awaited promises are being fulfilled (e.g., Matt. 13:16–17/Luke 10:23–24). Other statements of privilege, promise, or the importance of Jesus's actions give further reasons for celebration: something greater than the temple or Jonah or Solomon is here; Satan has fallen, and evil is being defeated; the disciples are blessed, for prophets and kings would have liked to see and hear what the disciples have seen and heard; there is no reason for fear, for the Father is pleased to give the kingdom to his people.[5] Fulfillment of the promises has come with Jesus.

Israel. The most difficult part of Jesus's message for us is its focus on Israel. For all his concern for the world, Jesus largely

5. E.g., Matt. 12:6, 41–42/Luke 11:31–32; Luke 10:17–24; and 12:32.

limits his ministry to Israel and only with reluctance turns his attention elsewhere.[6] Israel was supposed to be a blessing for all nations, but somewhere it got off track. Jesus does not attack Israel and certainly does not reject Israel or the temple. He confronts Israel, calls for repentance, warns *frequently* of judgment (despite all the focus on compassion), and, most importantly, reconstitutes Israel under his own leadership. What else could the appointment of twelve specific disciples be other than a symbol of the twelve sons of Jacob? In many ways Jesus embodies Israel in his own being and takes on the task of Israel as his own mission. Not surprisingly, except for "Lord," all the titles assigned to Jesus were previously titles of Israel: "Messiah," "Son of God," "Servant," and "Son of Man."[7] Jesus is the obedient Israel, the obedient Son of God.

Jesus's teaching about Israel comes mostly in parables or in warnings of judgment. The parables of the fig tree (Luke 13:6–9), the banquet (Matt. 22:1–14/Luke 14:15–24), the two sons (Matt. 21:28–32), the wicked tenants (Matt. 21:33–45/Mark 12:1–12/ Luke 20:9–18), and the ten pounds (Luke 19:11–27) are all specifically about Israel or its leaders. The lament over Jerusalem (Matt. 23:37–39/Luke 13:34–35), the cursing of the fig tree (Matt. 21:18–22/Mark 11:12–13), the temple incident (Matt. 21:12–17/ Mark 11:15–17/Luke 19:45–46/John 2:14–16), and warnings of the destruction of Jerusalem all underscore how much Jesus's mission is centered on Israel.

Without this focus on Israel and the conviction that God was fulfilling the promises to Israel, Jesus's call for celebration and his blessings of the "down and out" make no sense. To say "Blessed are the poor" (Matt. 5:3/Luke 6:20) is not good news; it is mockery unless something is happening to change the situation. Jesus is

6. Matthew 10:5–6; Matt. 8:5–13/Luke 7:1–10/John 4:46–54; and Matt. 15:21–28/ Mark 7:24–30.

7. E.g., with reference to Israel, "messiah" ("anointed") occurs in Ps. 89:38, "my son, my firstborn" in Exod. 4:22, "my servant" in Isa. 41:8, and "son of man" in Ps. 80:17.

convinced that in his own person God's promised intervention is in effect and the end-time promises are being fulfilled.

But where has Israel gone wrong? What is so wrong as to bring the warnings of judgment? Several factors could be listed, not least an inadequate understanding of the Torah. More importantly, Israel in large part has misunderstood the significance of election and has taken election as a privilege, leading to disdain for outsiders, but election has never been and is not now merely a privilege to be taken for granted. Election is always a responsibility and requires obedience *from the heart* to God's will.

Jesus warns that those who assume they will be at the messianic banquet might not be (Matt. 8:11–12/Luke 13:28–29; and Luke 14:15–24). With Jesus's coming, Israel faces a crisis. If the time of fulfillment is present, Israel is not ready. Jesus seeks to reorganize and redirect Israel and, in the end, to establish a new covenant. Jesus intends to gather a people—God will have a people—and prepare them to fulfill the role Israel was supposed to accomplish for the nations. His vision for Israel calls for repentance and a righteousness that goes to the core of one's being and does justice to God's intent for humanity.[8] It requires a focus on the love commands and a different understanding of what righteousness entails. In the end, Jesus's identification with Israel costs him his life. As righteous sufferers before him but in a much more significant way, he bears the judgment of Israel, giving himself for his people, but he is no mere martyr. He knows he is giving himself as a ransom for sins and to establish the promised new covenant,[9] a new way for people to be the people of God.

Perhaps part of our problem is that we think glibly about the promises to Israel. Fulfillment of those promises is at the heart of Jesus's message. If one thinks back on those promises, as evidenced briefly in the chapter on the gospel in the Old Testament, it

---

8. Note esp. the "Antitheses" in Matt. 5:13–48 and particularly the description of the disciples as the light of the world, surely drawing on Isa. 49:6.

9. Matthew 20:28/Mark 10:45; and Matt. 26:28/Mark 14:24/Luke 22:19–22.

is easy to see that the vision they hold out is stunningly beautiful—and exactly what human society needs. Jesus says it is present and coming with him.

Kingdom. The fourth feature of Jesus's gospel—and the basis of the other three—is the kingdom. Everyone knows that the "kingdom of God" (often in Matthew the "kingdom of heaven")[10] is important, but it frequently seems a vague term without content. If we are to understand Jesus's gospel (and that of the early church), understanding the kingdom is crucial. The kingdom is no less than *God coming as king* to defeat evil and establish righteousness—to put things right—in order to restore Israel in fulfillment of the Old Testament prophecies. *The kingdom is about God's participation with his people through the ministry of Jesus.*

The Old Testament kept pointing to a *vision* of what it would be like if God were truly king, if things were the way they were supposed to be. This vision anticipated what Israel and the world should be, and people longed for it. They still do today. Jesus comes saying in various ways, "The kingdom is here in my work and is in process." It is not for nothing that the charge above Jesus's head at the crucifixion reads, "This is Jesus, king of the Jews" (Matt. 27:37).

The kingdom is present with Jesus, but not in the way people expect. People assume God's coming will mean the defeat of their enemies, especially Rome, but God's coming always is twofold. It brings salvation *and* judgment, and Israel is judged first. If evil is to be defeated and righteousness established, Israel will need to repent and to learn just how deep obedience goes. Despite the Old Testament connections, *the God revealed in Jesus is a different kind of God*, one willing to identify with humanity as a servant and confront death. How do we hold together both "the crucified

---

10. On the distinction between "kingdom of heaven" and "kingdom of God" in Matthew, see Jonathan T. Pennington, *Heaven and Earth in the Gospel of Matthew*, Supplements to Novum Testamentum 126 (Leiden: Brill, 2007).

God"[11] as the very self-giving character of God and the exalted Lord who will judge and reign with power?

Jesus speaks about the kingdom in ways no one else has. No one else has spoken of the kingdom as already here or having drawn near, as coming, or as being sought, entered into, or seized. This *presence* of the kingdom is crucial in understanding Jesus, and it makes his message eschatological through and through. This is no message of mere ethical teaching. All of Jesus's ethic is rooted in eschatology. The concern is not going to heaven or the end of the world. The whole point of the gospel is that the kingdom— God's coming—is already at work in what Jesus is doing. Forgiveness is being handed out, people are being rescued, evil is being defeated, and God's love and goodness are on display—and you should live like it.

But there is still a "not yet" about the kingdom, as Jesus's instruction to pray "Your kingdom come" (Matt. 6:10) and numerous parables or sayings pointing to a future coming of the Son of Man attest. In fact, the *whole* of the Christian faith is framed on the pattern of now and not yet.[12] All the crucial words and ideas in Christian thought—the pouring out of the Spirit, justification, the new covenant, the inclusion of the gentiles—were realities expected for the end time, but the gospel says they are already present. The new age has erupted in the middle of the old, with the very presence of God revealed in Jesus, but the end is not yet. Followers of Jesus take their identity from this new age even while the old is still present. Do our churches know this?

The ethical demand of the kingdom is absolute. The presence of the kingdom *enormously* heightens the ethical challenge. Jesus asks people not merely to obey—as important as obedience is— but to be his disciples and follow him because of the kingdom.

---

11. Jürgen Moltmann, *The Crucified God*, trans. R. A. Wilson and John Bowden (New York: Harper & Row, 1974).

12. As obvious indicators of this pattern, see John's use of "The hour is coming and now is" (e.g., 4:23) or 1 John 3:2 ("We are *now* children of God, and it has *not yet* been revealed what we will be").

Jesus's ethical preaching calls people to the lifestyle the kingship of God requires. Although Jesus does not use "grace" language the way Paul does, we can summarize much of Jesus's preaching by saying, "The kingdom comes with limitless grace in the midst of an evil world, but with it comes limitless demand." Kingdom and the will of God go together, and Jesus, like the Old Testament before him and the church after him, offers no other standard for conduct than the character of God. He takes seriously that we are created in the image of God.

The Sermon on the Mount, which many readers view as too demanding and seek to avoid, is not law. It is the bright light of the gospel, which is to be, as well, a light to the nations. Who would not want to live in a community where people lived the Sermon on the Mount, where people avoided anger that demeans, sexual sins, and divorce; told the truth; did not seek revenge; and even loved their enemies? The sermon is the way God expects humans to live in response to the love and forgiveness brought by the kingdom. The character of the kingdom is derived from the God who is King—the God revealed in Jesus. Accordingly, the character of God's people is derived from the character of their God, as Matthew 5:48 underscores: "You will, therefore, be perfect as your heavenly Father is perfect."

Is Jesus's instruction too much, too demanding, too all-encompassing, and beyond what normal people can take? Is this for everybody, or just the "spiritual"? I do not intend to be elitist, but should we really cater to the least common denominator? Do not shrink from the command; its purpose is not to demand perfectionism but to emphasize that God's character is the only standard for human living. There is no "Christianity lite." You take the instruction for what it is or not at all.

The Sermon on the Mount is not too hard, not if you know from whom you come, to whom you are attached, and before whom you live. Knowing these things, could your life still be determined by anger, lust, unfaithfulness, lying, violence, and hate? Not a chance.

Jesus's message requires total commitment, but he does not call only the strong and successful. He calls everyone, including the weak, weary, and burdened, and the rest of the New Testament does too. He knows the weakness of humans and has compassion, but he knows no standard lower than the character of God and no extra level just for the clergy and the spiritual. The demands of self-denial, of cross-bearing in imitation of Jesus, of following him, of dying and rising are nonnegotiable. They are the message of the gospel and can be lived by anyone. Only there will we find life, joy, meaning, and strength given by God's Spirit, and it is the Spirit who makes such living possible for *all* of us.

The focus on compassion is not a focus on compassion without judgment. Judgment is a central feature of the kingdom proclamation. Accordingly, teaching about the future kingdom emphasizes a separation of the righteous from the evil (as with the parables of the wheat and weeds or of the net; Matt. 13:24–30, 47–50). Judgment is especially expressed for those who do not show compassion (as in the "parable" of the sheep and goats; Matt. 25:31–46), which is Jesus's chief complaint against the religious leaders.

Both the people of the Old Testament and Jews of first-century Palestine knew, celebration and God's compassion, but something different is happening with Jesus. Celebration and compassion receive the focus they do precisely because they are rooted in the fulfillment of the promises of Isaiah to Israel, in the coming of the King.

Luke 4:16-21 Summarizes Jesus's Gospel

Luke 4:16–21 summarizes not only Jesus's gospel but also his whole mission and his self-understanding. Luke thought so, for he placed this material as the beginning of Jesus's ministry.[13] In

---

13. Note that in Matthew (13:54–58) and Mark (6:1–6) the incident (without the quotation of Isa. 61) is placed more toward the center of their accounts.

effect he says, "If I tell you this story, you will know who Jesus is and what he is about." In addition, he tips his hand about what is significant for his own thought, for many of his favorite themes are developed from this text.

> And he went to Nazareth where he was raised, and as was his custom, on the Sabbath day he entered the synagogue, and then he stood to read. The book of the prophet Isaiah was given to him, and he unrolled the book and found the place where it is written, "The Spirit of the Lord is on me, because he anointed me to proclaim good news to the poor. He sent me to preach release to the captives and recovery of sight to the blind, to set the oppressed free, to preach the acceptable year of the Lord." When he had rolled up the book and given it to the attendant, he sat down, and the eyes of everyone in the synagogue were intently watching him. Then he began to say to them, "Today this Scripture has been fulfilled in your hearing."[14]

Why did Jesus select this text, and why were people intently watching him? Because the text Jesus read was Isaiah 61—actually, Isaiah 61 and phrases from other parts of Isaiah.[15] As indicated earlier, this is one of the key Old Testament promises, and for Jesus's hearers Isaiah 61 was *a highly charged text about the Messiah*. One of the Dead Sea Scrolls connects Isaiah 61, "the last days," Isaiah 52:7 (the good news of God's salvation and reign), and the Jubilee (the ultimate symbol of release and forgiveness, based in Leviticus 25). The text of 11Q Melchizedek, column II, asserts:

> And as for what he said: [[Lev. 25:13]] "In this year of jubilee, you shall return, each one, to his respective property" . . . Its interpretation for the last days refers to the captives, . . . and they are the

14. The word *aphesis* occurs two times in what Jesus read, once translated as "release" and once as "free." Elsewhere the word is used for forgiveness, the release from sins.

15. Luke's form of the quotation of Isa. 61 adds recovery of sight, apparently from Isa. 42:7, an addition in the Septuagint as well. These words could come from Isa. 35:5 or Ps. 146:7–8. Luke's form also adds letting the oppressed go free (literally "with release") from Isa. 58:6.

inheritance of Melchizedek, who will make them return. [[Isa. 61:1]] And liberty will be proclaimed for them to free them from the debt of all their iniquities. . . . This . . . is the day of peace about which he said . . . through Isaiah the prophet, who said: [[Isa. 52:7]] "How beautiful upon the mountains are the feet of the messenger who announces peace, the messenger of good who announces salvation, saying to Zion: "your God reigns." Its interpretation: . . . And the messenger is the anointed of the spirit . . . And the messenger of good who announces salvation is the one about whom it is written . . . [[Isa. 61:2]] "to comfort the afflicted."[16]

Do not let the brackets, added to indicate the source of quotations, or my omitting, to save space, parts of the manuscript lead you astray. This passage is crucial evidence underscoring the importance of Isaiah 61 in first-century Palestine. Jesus had the audacity to say that Isaiah 61, this end-time and messianic text full of promise, was fulfilled with him. He did not say, "I am the Messiah," and he seems mostly to have avoided the word, no doubt because his view of Messiah did not fit that of the people. Still, with this text he clearly was making an unprecedented claim to be God's anointed one, God's agent to bring in the end-time Jubilee. The themes of compassion and fulfillment are obviously rooted in this text. This is the good news: the one anointed with God's Spirit has come to bring freedom and comfort for the poor and oppressed. He is here now. You can see why people were intently watching him and were astonished by what he said.

The importance of Isaiah 61 for Jesus's own self-understanding is shown by two other texts. First, in Matthew 11:2–6/Luke 7:18–23, John the Baptist sends messengers to ask if Jesus was "the one to come, or are we waiting for someone else?" Jesus's reply is, "Tell John what you have seen and heard: the blind recovering

16. Double brackets mark off the identification of the Old Testament texts cited. A number of words have been restored because of gaps in the manuscript. See Florentino García Martínez and Eibert J. C. Tigchelaar, *The Dead Sea Scrolls Study Edition* (Leiden: Brill, 1998), 2:1206–7.

sight, the lame walking, lepers being cleansed, the deaf hearing, the dead being raised,[17] and the poor being told the good news." He might as well say, "Tell John that Isaiah 61 is being fulfilled." Second, the Beatitudes in Matthew 5:3–5 are framed on Isaiah 61:1–2: "Blessed are the poor in spirit. . . . Blessed are those who mourn." Isaiah 61 is one of the most important texts forming Jesus's own self-understanding.

Other people have preached deliverance, but Jesus preaches that it is present now. The kingdom of God is at hand with him; the banquet is ready. Even now God's lost children may sit down at the table with their Father and Creator—and Judge, a remarkable image of grace.[18] If the focus is on deliverance now, response to Jesus or at least to his message is crucial. He presents a crisis to the nation, even though parts of his message seem to forestall judgment. People seek release from Rome; Jesus speaks of a greater release, from indebtedness to God. Rome's claim to power does not deserve direct attack, even as it is being set aside. For Jesus the release offered in his message is much more generally the release from the human plight of suffering, sin, and evil. That release is still needed today as much as ever.

Another feature from Isaiah 61 is obviously important—the endowment with the Spirit. The promise was that at the end the Spirit would be poured out (e.g., Joel 2:28–32 [Hebrew 3:1–5]). All the evangelists emphasize that the Spirit is the key both to Jesus's identity and to the kingdom. For Matthew and Luke, that starts with Jesus's conception, and with all four evangelists it is the major feature of Jesus's baptism. The proof of the kingdom's

17. 4Q521 2 II, 7–13, in speaking of the Messiah, also connects Isa. 61:1 and raising the dead: "For he will honour the pious upon the throne of an eternal kingdom, freeing prisoners, giving sight to the blind, straightening out the twisted. . . . And the Lord will perform marvellous acts such as have not existed, just as he said for he will heal the badly wounded and he will make the dead live, he will proclaim good news to the poor and . . . enrich the hungry." Martínez and Tigchelaar, *Dead Sea Scrolls Study Edition*, 2:1044–45.

18. This language has its origin partly in Joachim Jeremias, *The Eucharistic Words of Jesus*, trans. Norman Perrin (London: SCM, 1966), 262.

presence is the working of the Spirit, and the only reason the church can call Jesus the Christ, the Anointed One, is because of their conviction that he was anointed with the Spirit. In the life of the early church, the Spirit became the origin and essential ingredient of Christian existence.[19] It still is.

Jesus's Gospel as Revelation

One other aspect of Jesus's gospel is clear: his gospel is a revelation from the Father. Revelation is another essential ingredient of the gospel; without revelation from God opening the eyes of the blind, there is no good news.[20] In the next chapter we will see that the Prologue of John presents Jesus as the ultimate revelation of God. The Synoptics do not have as much explicit emphasis on revelation, but it is still a prominent theme, obviously so in the birth narratives, with angelic messengers. Even in Mark, the mystery—the revelation—of the kingdom is given to disciples, Jesus offers new and authoritative teaching, and his teaching is like new wine that cannot fit in old wineskins.[21] Then, in something of a climax, Matthew and Luke both have the Johannine "bolt from the blue," the revelation saying in Matthew 11:25–27/ Luke 10:21–22 that sounds so much like John's Christology: "All things have been handed over to me by my Father, and no one knows the son except the Father, nor does anyone know the Father except the son and anyone to whom the son chooses to reveal him." The good news is that Jesus has come to show what God is really like.

19. See, e.g., Matt. 12:18, 28; John 3:3–8; Rom. 8:1–17, esp. v. 9; Titus 3:5; and 1 John 4:13.
20. On the gospel as revelation, see Klyne Snodgrass, "The Gospel in Romans: A Theology of Revelation," in *Gospel in Paul: Studies on Corinthians, Galatians and Romans for Richard N. Longenecker*, ed. L. Ann Jervis and Peter Richardson (Sheffield: Sheffield Academic, 1994), 288–314.
21. See Mark 1:27 (Luke 4:32); 2:22 (Matt. 9:17/Luke 5:37–38); and 4:11 (Matt. 13:11/Luke 8:10).

Did Jesus's Gospel Emphasize Participation?

The simple answer is a resounding "Yes!" Participation is perhaps less obvious in the Synoptics than John, but it is still front and center. Part of the difference is due to the Synoptics focusing more on the confrontation with Israel while John, who still has that confrontation, is more concerned with the life Jesus communicates to his followers.

God's participation with humanity is, of course, emphasized. That is what the incarnation is about. The compassion Jesus shows and the kingdom itself are about God coming to participate with his people. Jesus gives himself as a ransom for people (Matt. 20:28) and his body and blood for forgiveness of sins (26:26–28). The depth of the divine participation with humanity is revealed in the striking statement "Whatever you did to one of these least brothers and sisters of mine, you did to me" (25:40). This is serious identification and participation on the part of God with us.

Still other texts emphasize the care of God for his people and his eagerness to forgive and to seek the lost. Disciples are assured that God's Spirit will supply language for their defense when one is on trial for faith. All this says again, "God is for us," and seeks a people who will live with God and draw sustenance from him. The gospel is always, and always has been, a gospel of participation.

Participation appears in other texts as well, especially in Matthew's Gospel. This whole Gospel is framed on the presence of God: Immanuel, God with us, in 1:23; "Where two or three are gathered unto my name, I am there in their midst" in 18:20; and "I am with you always" in 28:20. In 11:28–30 the burdened are invited to come to Jesus to find rest, to take on his yoke—participate with him—and learn from him. This closeness *is* and enables discipleship in keeping with Jesus's frequent call to action and obedience. Such participation excludes passivity. God's participation with humans *is* the good news.

The human part in participation is also emphasized. If John stresses union with Christ, the Synoptics' stress is much more on following Jesus, and *it is no less an attachment to him*. (Of course, John also emphasizes following Jesus; see, e.g., 1:43; 10:4–27; 12:26; and 21:19–22.)

The classic statement on discipleship occurs with variations seven times across the four Gospels. Matthew 16:24–25 is one example: "Then Jesus said to his disciples, 'If anyone wants to come after me, let that person deny self, take up his or her cross, and continually follow me. Whoever wants to save life loses it, and whoever loses life because of me will save it.'"[22] Denial of self is not denial of things to self; it is the refusal to find life in one's own desires, resources, and goals and the choice to find life in obedience to God's will by following Jesus. To deny self and take up one's cross is a renunciation of an ego-centered life—the breaking of every link that ties a person to himself or herself. It is not about pain and suffering common to all humans. It is identification with Jesus's death (and resurrection) for the purposes of living like him and doing his ministry, and it is the equivalent of what Paul means with dying and rising with Christ. For both Jesus and Paul, discipleship and faith mean being displaced from oneself and being attached to Jesus.

Making observations about Jesus, reflecting on Jesus, and admiring Jesus are not enough. Søren Kierkegaard rejects both observing or reflecting on and being an admirer of Christ instead of a follower. You can observe and reflect on Jesus, admire him from a distance, and sit safely without any real engagement with him or involvement in his purposes. A follower seeks to be what he or she admires. Kierkegaard argues Jesus's life was calculated to require followers and to make admirers impossible, and he asserts that only the follower, the imitator, is the true Christian.[23] Without question, he is correct.

22. The other six are in Matt. 10:38–39; Mark 8:34–38; Luke 9:23–27; 14:27 (and the whole of 14:25–33); 17:33; and John 12:25.

23. Søren Kierkegaard, *Practice in Christianity*, ed. and trans. Howard V. Hong and Edna H. Hong, Kierkegaard's Writings 20 (Princeton: Princeton University Press,

Following Jesus is an engagement with him that changes identity. Christians take their identity from their Lord headed to the cross. Lest this seem dreary and morbid, remember that the discipleship saying is about giving up on one form of life to gain another and *better* life. Jesus announced that people find life by giving up on it and then finding it in direct connection with following him. Part of the *good news* is that you find life by losing it. Jesus's gospel entails and demands the defeat of self-centeredness. It is a gospel of transformation above all else. You do not have to be self-centered, alone and without meaning, and dominated by evil, and that is good news, precisely what humans need.

Further, if Christianity is framed on the new age breaking into the old, on the presence of the future in Jesus Christ, why do people still take their identity from the old age instead of the new? Shouldn't we live like we believe that something new and reorienting has arrived?

So, what is the gospel in the Synoptic Gospels? It is that God, in Jesus, has come to fulfill his covenant promises, to reign as king and live *with* his people, to give them real life in relation with him, and to enable them to be who they are supposed to be. All this is enhanced and spelled out in the rest of the New Testament, especially with regard to the significance of Jesus's death and resurrection and the pouring out of the Spirit.

1991), 233–58, esp. 236, 240, 254. Some translations of Kierkegaard use forms of the word "reflect," and some "observe."

six

Deep Participation in John and 1 John

God comes to people who have nothing but room for God—and this hollow space, this emptiness in people is called in Christian speech, faith. . . . That is the meaning of Good Friday and Easter Sunday: the way of God to people leads back to God.

Dietrich Bonhoeffer[1]

The Gospel of John is of a different nature than the Synoptics, but this Gospel grounds and heightens nearly every aspect of the Synoptic message, although shifts in emphasis occur, evidenced most obviously in the absence of narrative parables and in kingdom language being used sparsely.

John's Prologue is by far the most explicit of the Gospel prologues. In the first verse Jesus is recognized as God, the same substance as God, and 1:14–18 uses the story of Moses seeking a revelation of God (Exod. 33–34), in many ways *the* paradigmatic text on revelation, to convey powerfully the identity of

1. Dietrich Bonhoeffer, "Jesus Christ and the Essence of Christianity," trans. Geffrey B. Kelly, in *A Testament to Freedom: The Essential Writings of Dietrich Bonhoeffer*, ed. Geffrey B. Kelly and F. Burton Nelson (San Francisco: HarperCollins, 1990), 52–53.

Jesus. He is the ultimate revelation of the Father, the incarnate Word embodying the grace and truth so characteristic of God (Exod. 34:6). He is the unique God,[2] who is in the closest possible relation to the Father, who has revealed God to humanity, and who came in flesh to live among them—that is, to participate with humans (John 1:14–18). This is the Johannine version of Immanuel, God with us. By the end of the first chapter, John has used almost every lofty title or description of Jesus: God, Lamb of God who takes away the sin of the world, the one baptizing with the Spirit, Son of God, Rabbi, Messiah/Christ, King of Israel, and Son of Man. No doubt about Jesus's identity remains as the story is told.

The focus on revelation reappears in many ways throughout John's Gospel. Jesus is the one who hears and sees the Father, and what he has heard and seen he communicates to his followers.[3] The one who has seen him has seen the Father (John 14:9).

The *real* gospel is continually expressed throughout the book, and repeatedly, connection to Jesus and the Spirit is emphasized as the source of life and nourishment for life. Rebirth is required for involvement in the kingdom, but rebirth language occurs only in 1:13 and 3:1–8, appearing a total of nine times. The image of rebirth is infrequent in Scripture,[4] and it is merely another way of expressing what other language—such as denying self, taking up a cross and following, and dying and rising with Christ—communicates in explaining the gospel.

---

2. The best and earliest manuscripts in John 1:18 have *monogenēs theos ho ōn eis ton kolpon tou patros*, "the unique God who is in the bosom of the Father."

3. See John 3:31–35; 5:17–30; 10:15, 30, 38; 12:49–50; and a great deal of chaps. 14–17.

4. First John also uses *gennan* ("give birth to") ten times, all with reference to birth from God (2:29; 3:9 [2x]; 4:7; and 5:1 [3x], 4, 18 [2x]). Outside the Johannine writings no New Testament writer uses the simple verb *gennan* to speak of rebirth from God, and other expressions for rebirth are rare. *Anagennan* is used in 1 Pet. 1:3, 23 to express rebirth, and *artigennētos* is used in 2:2 as a figure of speech referring to Christians. *Palingenesia* occurs only at Matt. 19:28 (with reference to end-time restoration) and at Titus 3:5 (of regeneration). The only other occurrence of rebirth language is James 1:18, which uses *apokyein*.

There are actually five references to rebirth in John 3:3–8:[5] "born from above" (v. 3), "born from water and Spirit" (v. 5), "born from the Spirit" (v. 6), "born from above" (v. 7), and "born from the Spirit" (v. 8).[6] They all mean the same thing, a new beginning and transformation brought about by God's Spirit. Verse 6 is striking: "That born from the flesh [i.e., the merely human] is flesh; that born from the Spirit is spirit"[7]—that is, it *takes on the quality of the Spirit*. The focus is on both participation and transformation.

The Gospel of John has such an enormous emphasis on participation that it is difficult to talk about its good news apart from participation. This Gospel, and 1 John as well, is overwhelmingly about a deep participation with the God revealed in Jesus. It is about God filling that emptiness to which Bonhoeffer referred in the quotation at the start of the chapter. The participation of God is stressed in the incarnation and the repeated emphasis on the fact that Jesus comes from the Father and that believers are those who are bound to, united with, Jesus.

John is the Gospel of union with Christ, most obviously in John 15 and other texts that use the Greek word *menein*, which conveys the idea of *remaining in* or abiding in / staying in Christ. This word occurs forty times in the Gospel and twenty-four more in 1 John.[8] It can be used merely of staying in a particular place, but it is often used in profound and theologically significant ways. It is used of the Spirit remaining on Jesus (1:32–33), of the Father remaining in Jesus (14:10), of a complaint that God's word does not remain in people (5:38), of people remaining in Jesus's word (8:31), of the Spirit remaining in people (14:17), of people

5. I draw here on my article "That Which Is Born from ΠΝΕΥΜΑ [*PNEUMA*] Is ΠΝΕΥΜΑ [*PNEUMA*]: Rebirth and Spirit in John 3:5–6," in *Perspectives on John: Method and Interpretation in the Fourth Gospel*, ed. Robert Sloan and Mikeal C. Parsons (Lewiston, NY: Edwin Mellen, 1993), 181–205.

6. Excluding Nicodemus's two uses of birth language in v. 4 and "born from the flesh" in v. 6.

7. Or should that second occurrence of "spirit" be capitalized, as in Moffatt's translation?

8. Plus three in 2 John and one in Revelation.

remaining in Christ's love (15:9–10), and, most important of all, of Jesus remaining in people and people remaining in him (6:56)—being as closely attached to him as a branch to a vine (15:3–7); that is, being part of him and drawing life from him.[9]

The five occurrences of *menein* in John 1:32–39 are especially revealing. The first two refer to the Spirit coming upon Jesus at his baptism and remaining on him (vv. 32–33). The three occurrences in verses 38–39 may seem mundane, but they are not, if one has Johannine antennae at all. Two of John the Baptist's disciples follow Jesus because of the Baptist's witness. When Jesus sees them following, he asks, "What are you seeking?" Their reply is, "Rabbi, where are you remaining [*menein*]?" On the surface it seems they ask, "At which motel are you staying?" but much more is going on. Jesus's reply is, "Come and see." All three of these expressions—what one seeks, where one remains, and the invitation to come and see—become themes that recur throughout the book. The disciples go with Jesus and see where he is staying, but one does not really know where Jesus stays[10]—remains—until chapters 14–17, where Jesus is described as in the Father and the Father as in him (14:10; 17:5, 11–23). As we will see a bit later, believers are invited into the relation the Son has with the Father, into the very life of the triune God.

This participation of believers with Jesus—and the Father, because of Jesus's unity with him—is so intimate that the whole of one's existence is housed in and determined by him. One lives in him, and he lives in the believer. One's internal and external life is determined by this close attachment to Jesus. Remaining in Christ means Christ is the source of life; one draws life from him, or in the words of 6:56–57, the one who eats his flesh and drinks his blood remains in him and is nourished thereby.

9. The unity of the Father, Jesus, and the disciples is underscored with other language in chap. 17.

10. *Menein* can be used merely of staying at a specific place, as in 4:40, but the exchange in 1:39 is much more loaded with Johannine double meaning.

Believing in the Gospel of John

What establishes this intimacy of relation? Surely the Spirit is the agent creating the relation, but human believing is crucial. In John believing has a special dimension. John will not allow believing to be conceived of as something mental. The verb for "believe" (*pisteuein*) occurs ninety-eight times in the Fourth Gospel, but the noun "faith" (*pistis*) *never* occurs. It is as if the noun is too static, whereas the verb is dynamic and reflects the action believing requires.[11] More importantly, thirty-six times John uses "believe into" (*pisteuein eis*), a construction that sounds clumsy in both Greek and English and *does not occur in secular Greek or in the Septuagint*. Elsewhere in the New Testament this construction occurs only eight times, several of which seem to be confessional.[12] Are these other occurrences due to the influence of the Johannine tradition? In any case, as important as believing certain facts about Jesus is, John understands believing as something much more profound. The preposition *eis* connotes direction, as with going into a house, or the purpose for which something is done. Translations do not do justice to "believe into," usually rendering it merely as "believe in," but the expression must be taken with all seriousness. Believing into involves *movement into* a close association with Jesus, a commitment to, an attachment to, and a participation with him.[13] With such believing, passivity is impossible. With such attachment to and participation with Christ, one must act and live in keeping with the character of Christ. The primary way this happens is by love. This kind of believing is what "remaining in" is all about, and all this is very close to Paul's "in Christ" thinking.

11. Similarly, the verb "know" (*ginōskein*) occurs fifty-seven times, but the noun *gnōsis* not at all.

12. Matthew 18:6; Acts 10:43; 14:23; Gal. 2:16; Phil. 1:29; 1 Pet. 1:8; and 1 John 5:10, 13. Mark 9:42 has this reading as a textual variant. "Belief into" (*pistis eis*), using the noun, occurs in Acts 20:21; 24:24; 26:18; Col. 2:5; and 1 Pet. 1:21.

13. The one text where this seems less the case is John 2:23. People believed because of the signs they saw, but their believing was inadequate. Cf. John 14:11.

Images of Participation

John has other compelling ways to communicate participation. One of the most graphic portrays Jesus as the bread of life and calls for eating Jesus's flesh and drinking his blood (John 6:33–58). He is also the source of water for the thirsty (4:10–14; 6:35; 7:37–38). These are strong images to convey that Jesus is the source of life and that his being determines life. In chapter 10 we will return to this theme of ingesting Christ or God, for it is not merely John who uses it.[14] It is a major theme in Scripture.

Jesus is also the Good Shepherd who calls his sheep by name, leads them, and gives his life for them (John 10:1–18) so that they may have life abundantly. The Farewell Discourses underscore that Jesus, via the Spirit, will be with his disciples. *He will not leave them as orphans* (14:18). Instead, for the person who loves him and keeps his word, "My Father will love that person, and we will come and make a home with that person" (14:23). This is a strong family image of participation.

Chapter 17 is in many ways a climactic description of participation, and here the invitation into the life of the triune God is clear. The above quotations from church fathers about sharing in the divine nature derive partly from this text.[15] Eternal life is described not as going to heaven but as knowing God and Jesus whom he sent (v. 3). This is not theoretical knowledge, knowing about Jesus. It is relational knowledge, knowing him experientially. Jesus's unity with the Father, their mutual indwelling, and their common mission summarize what this Gospel seeks to communicate about the identity of Jesus. Jesus's disciples are drawn into this unity, into this mutual indwelling, and into this ministry (note vv. 18–23). Verse 21 is especially revealing: ". . . that they all may be one, even as you, Father, are in me and I am in you, that they may also be in us." This is a breathtaking description of participation.

14. See pp. 153–56.
15. See pp. 27–29.

Everywhere the message is the same. God is for us and draws us into solidarity through Christ so that we live with God and are engaged in the purposes of God.

The purpose of all this participation is that transformation of life may occur. It is not merely that people may go to heaven, a topic never mentioned in John. It is about life in the present *and in the future*, but the avenue to that life is attachment to the God revealed in Jesus. Such attachment will not leave us as before or allow passivity; by necessity, participation with the triune God transforms life. The Word comes as the true light enlightening all (John 1:9), those who are born of the Spirit take on the character of the Spirit (3:6), Jesus came that people may have life *in abundance* (10:10), and they are commanded to "believe into" the light so that they may be children of the light (12:36)—that is, people who have the characteristics of the light. Participatory faith will not leave you as you were.

Participation in 1 John

First John is also overwhelmingly about participation. The first chapter is largely about *koinōnia* ("sharing," "participation"; see vv. 3, 6, 7). The author and those with him seek to draw the readers into a participation with them, but that also means a participation with the Father and with his Son, Jesus Christ. This first chapter emphasizes that one takes on the characteristics of that with which one participates. If you participate with God, you by necessity are marked by the characteristics of God. This is the primary message of the book. You cannot participate with God and live in the opposite direction. No, participation with God means "walking in the light" and doing the truth *and* continually being cleansed from sin so as to live as God intended humans to live (1:6–9).

The *koinōnia* language does not appear in the rest of the book; rather, *menein* ("remain") takes over the task of communicating participation. The first of the twenty-four occurrences—all in

chapters 2 through 4—in 2:6, underscores what we have already
seen: the one claiming to remain in Christ should live the same
way Christ lived. There can be nothing passive about participation. An equally heavy focus is given to being honest with yourself
about whether you are indeed living as you say. As these three
chapters unfold, the gospel message is emphasized, as it was in
chapter 1, so that remaining in the Father and the Son requires
remaining in the gospel message. This brings emphasis on God's
role in enabling participation with humanity. First John emphasizes the love of God repeatedly: that God loved first, that Jesus
is from the Father and has come in the flesh, that he gave himself
for our sins, and that he is engaged with us, hearing our prayers
and responding to them.[16]

Worth noting as well is that, while only seven times Paul has
the idea of being in God,[17] the Johannine material has both "in
God" and "in Christ," seemingly without concern for any difference.[18] In 1 John remaining in God/Christ, with life being shaped
accordingly, is key to confidence for living and at judgment day
(2:28–29). The Christian can expect to be made like Christ at his
second coming, but that hope has a present impact so that people
take action now to live holy lives because he is holy (3:2–3, 7).

Remaining in Christ obviously is the same as Paul's "in Christ"
thinking, but the implications are more forcefully drawn in 1 John.
Here the author insists that the one remaining in Christ *is not
sinning and is not able to continue sinning*, for God's "seed" (his
word) remains in him or her (3:6, 9; 5:18). How can the author
be so confident—or is it just too extreme? He takes seriously that
participation with Christ, the very character of believing, must
bring transformation in one's life. He is not speaking of perfectionism, for already at 1:8 and 10 he has insisted that people,
believers too, both have sin—sin is part of their being—and have

16. See 1 John 3:1, 5, 16; 4:2, 7–11, 14–19; and 5:14–15.
17. See p. 18, n. 17.
18. E.g., John 3:21; 17:21, 23; 1 John 2:6; 4:4, 12–16; and 5:20.

sinned. He has encouraged people to confess sins, knowing that God forgives and cleanses. The verbs in 3:6–9 about not sinning are present tense, designating an ongoing process. The point is that people remaining in Christ cannot go on living a life of sin. They cannot, if God's word has taken root in them. *Participation with Christ makes it harder to sin!* You cannot easily be conscious of being attached to Christ and choose to sin anyway. The Old Testament already shows this thinking: the evil "do not set God before them" (Ps. 86:14). It is hard to sin if you are conscious of God in your life. Instead of sin, life is marked by love, as the verses following in 1 John 3 show.

Participation with God Results in Love

Without love there is no relation to God, but love is not some amorphous feeling or something conjured from ourselves. This love mirrors the love of the Father—*and* the commands of the Father.[19] Love is demonstrated by obedience, as it also is in John's Gospel (see, e.g., John 14:15, 21). In parallel with Paul's spheres-of-influence thinking, the author sees believers as transferred from one realm to another, from death *into* life (1 John 3:14).[20] The proof that one has been transferred from one sphere to another is love for the brothers and sisters. It is impossible to separate salvation and ethics.

The connection between love and remaining in God and Christ appears compellingly in 4:12–16, and with it several other important themes. The statement that no one has ever seen God (v. 12) repeats a major biblical conviction beginning with Moses's mountain experience, when he is allowed to see only God's "back" (Exod. 33–34). Passages stressing that no one has seen God or expressing fear of death for anyone who does are often directly

---

19. See 1 John 2:3–8; 3:22–24; 4:21; and 5:2–3.
20. The same language is in John 5:24, and Col. 1:13 has the same idea expressed with slightly different language.

about revelation of God, as in the passage in Exodus.[21] We saw that John's Gospel Prologue, in direct allusion to Exodus 33–34 and Moses's experience, says that no one has ever seen God but that the incarnate Word, the unique God, who is in the closest possible relation to the Father, has revealed him (John 1:14–18).[22] What is clear in 1 John 4:12–21 is that while no one has seen God, "we" have seen Jesus, the very revelation of God, and we have seen our brothers and sisters. This christological-revelation thinking starts the letter in 1:1–3: we have seen the one from the beginning, the one from the Father. First John 4:12–21 now takes this revelation thinking deeper and gives it both an ethical turn and a participation emphasis. Those who love others and confess that Jesus is the Son of God are given God's Spirit, and they remain in God, and God remains in them. No one has seen God, but we *have seen other people*. If we love, God remains in us, and his love is completed in us (cf. 3:17, which asks how God's love can be remaining in someone who closes off compassion to someone in need).

The assurance that one remains in God and God in that person is the Holy Spirit (1 John 4:13; 3:24). The Spirit is, in fact, the means by which participation happens. Then, as with Paul, humans take an active role in participation by affirming with word and action that Jesus is the Son of God. In these verses the role of the triune God is brought to light. It is all summarized by God's love for humans and their love mirroring his, by confession of Jesus Christ and life with him enabled by the Spirit, and it is described repeatedly with the language of remaining in God and he in us—participation.[23]

As elsewhere in Scripture, the gospel is about God's participation with us, being for us, sending his Son and revealing himself,

---

21. See, e.g., Gen. 28:16–17; Exod. 20:18–19; 33:20; Deut. 5:24–27; Judg. 6:22–23; and Isa. 6:5.

22. See pp. 91–92.

23. Like the Fourth Gospel, 1 John uses "believe into" (*pisteuein eis*) in 5:10, 13. In the former, "believing into" Christ results in God's message being rooted in one's being; in the latter, it results in eternal life.

dealing with our sin, and giving the Spirit to enable life with God and bring transformation. It is about participation from top to bottom. The gospel cannot be conceived of apart from this close association with God, and if that is so, life cannot go on as if God were not there.

seven

The Gospel in the Book of Acts

If my affirmation of the facts of Jesus' death and resurrection is not one that sweeps my whole existence into its power, I am not making an affirmation of faith in the biblical sense.

Lewis Smedes[1]

Acts is different. The gospel in Acts is not the gospel in the Gospels. It could not be, given the cataclysmic events of the crucifixion and resurrection, which are only narrated in the Gospels and not explained. In fairness, they are not explained in Acts either. Acts gives relatively little attention to *explaining* the significance of the death of Jesus, and even though it gives enormous emphasis to his resurrection and ascension, the theology of the resurrection and ascension is not developed in any detailed way either. It is as if the significance of the death, resurrection, and ascension of Jesus is self-evident. What made them so for Luke's readers? The gospel in Acts is also not the same as the gospel in Paul's Letters or the Johannine writings, even though all of them point to the

---

1. Lewis B. Smedes, *Union with Christ: A Biblical View of New Life in Jesus Christ* (Grand Rapids: Eerdmans, 1983), 143.

death and resurrection of Jesus as the center of the good news
and the basis of transformation. The Gospels, the Pauline Letters,
and the Johannine writings do not emphasize the ascension the
same way Acts does.

The gospel in Acts is expressed mostly in the speeches and
sermons and in the narrative summaries. Because the speeches
and sermons address different groups and have different purposes,
the gospel is expressed in a variety of ways. Sometimes speeches
in Acts have other purposes and are not intended to express the
gospel. In such texts the gospel is muted or hardly even present,
as with Paul's address in Athens (17:22–31) or Stephen's speech
(7:2–56).

The differences between the presentation of the gospel in the
Gospels, Acts, John, and Paul should not be ignored, but significant continuity is present too. (See the appendix on the relation of
the gospel of Jesus and the gospel of Paul.) Acts, not surprisingly,
stands as a bridge between the Gospels and Paul's Letters, even
though Acts is later than Paul's Letters. Like the Gospels, Acts
places emphasis on the *historical ministry of the earthly Jesus*,
something Paul's Letters do not do. For example, Peter tells Cornelius and his household:

> He [God] sent the message to the children of Israel, preaching
> peace through Jesus Christ—this one is Lord of all. *You know
> what happened in the whole of Judea, beginning from Galilee
> with the baptism John preached, how God anointed Jesus from
> Nazareth with the Holy Spirit and power. He went about doing
> good and healing all those overpowered by the devil, because God
> was with him. And we are witnesses of all the things he did both
> in the country of the Jews and in Jerusalem.* They killed him by
> hanging him on a tree. This one God raised on the third day and
> caused him to be seen, not by all the people but by witnesses picked
> beforehand by God, to us who ate with him and drank with him
> after he was raised from the dead. He commanded us to preach to
> the people and to testify that this is the one appointed by God to

judge both the living and the dead. All the prophets testify about
this one that everyone believing in him receives forgiveness of sins
through his name. (Acts 10:36–43)

Paul's Letters give little attention to the italicized emphases, even
though he no doubt agreed. But in Acts, Jesus *of Nazareth* is the
focus of the gospel, even if details about him or his teaching are
sparse. God worked through Jesus, and he is the one who brings
salvation.

Several items in this Acts 10 passage, which has to be judged
one of the most important expressions of the gospel anywhere,
merit attention. Peace is offered as a summary of the gospel. Paul
would agree wholeheartedly, as texts like Ephesians 2:14–18 and
other passages on reconciliation show. Peace is in many ways the
foundational idea of the gospel—peace with God, with other
people, and within ourselves. If our proclamation of the gospel
is not focused on peace, it is not the gospel of the New Testament.

This passage emphasizes as well Jesus as Lord, the participation
of God with humans through Jesus, the role of the Holy Spirit, the
resurrection of Jesus, judgment, and forgiveness of sins. Forgiveness is not a big part of Paul's thinking, for he is more concerned
with sin as a tyrant, and people need freedom, not just forgiveness,
from the tyrant.[2] For Luke, however, forgiveness is a major focus.
Although they treat it with different language, *all* the biblical
writers presume sin is a major problem that must be dealt with,
remedied, and displaced. Without that, there is no good news.

A narrative of God's work throughout history and especially
with Israel is the foundation for presenting the gospel, and Acts
recounts this history several times (7:2–53; 13:16–41; 14:15–17;
and 17:22–31). Clearly Luke thinks his readers need to know the
whole of God's story. God's promises from long ago are now being
fulfilled with Jesus. Miracles are often mentioned when people tell

---

2. This does not mean Paul is not concerned with sins. Quite the contrary is true,
as the whole of 1 Corinthians and the vice lists in his letters show.

about Jesus's earthy ministry, or a miracle effected by the risen Lord accompanies the telling of the gospel.[3] The emphasis on the life of Jesus does not mean there is less focus on Christology—quite the contrary. Especially because of the resurrection, but also because of the Scriptures, Jesus is shown to be the Christ, the Servant, the Lord, the Son of God, and the origin of life.

Other obvious connections between Acts and the gospel in the Gospels are repentance and forgiveness, which are a focus with both John the Baptist and Jesus.[4] In Acts, repentance and forgiveness of sins are nearly always dominant ideas when the gospel is presented. Repentance in the New Testament is not merely a change of mind; it is more in keeping with the Old Testament idea of turning to the Lord. In 20:21 repentance is explicitly "toward God" and is joined with faith "toward our Lord Jesus." In 26:20 Paul summarizes his preaching as telling people to repent, turn to God, and do works in keeping with repentance. The notion that repentance and faith are merely mental would never occur to the early church. Turning to Jesus involves transformation and obedience, and any idea that faith is not necessarily transformative would have been preposterous.

Perhaps it is worth stopping at this point to reflect on our own society and churches. If the Gospels and Acts focus on sins and forgiveness, why is there so little focus on, or even mention of, sins now? Throughout the church's history, especially with Martin Luther and the Great Awakenings, sins were the problem being addressed. Are churches today even addressing any problem? Why bother with forgiveness unless there is awareness of sin, moral failure, shortcomings, and the consequences? We do not speak much of judgment, but if there is no judgment, why should there be concern for salvation and for change? Such questions raise the

---

3. See Acts 2:22; 3:13, 15; 4:11–12, 27; 5:42; 8:12, 35; 9:5; 10:36–38; 11:20; and 13:32.

4. Salvation from sin and forgiveness of sins are present right from the birth narratives to the resurrection appearances. The concern for sins is evident not only in explicit occurrences of the word "sin" but, even more, in Jesus's ethical teaching.

issue of the identity of the modern church. Who are these people, why are they bothering to come together, and why should anyone join them? On the other hand, evil is as prevalent as it ever was, and perhaps more so. The need for the gospel is as great as ever.

Another connection between the Gospels and Acts is of major importance, and it is the way Acts continues the focus from Jesus's ministry on the kingdom. The risen Lord teaches about the kingdom (1:3). At several points the gospel is summarized as preaching about the kingdom or, more explicitly, about Jesus and the kingdom.[5] Acts ends with Paul in Rome, preaching the kingdom and teaching the things about Jesus, with all boldness and unhindered (28:31). The gospel of the early church and the focus on death and resurrection went hand in hand with the reality of the kingdom. The resurrection is a result of God's kingdom activity.

The connections between the gospel in Acts and the gospel in Paul should not be overlooked either. Unlike the Gospels and most of the non-Pauline writings, Acts, like Paul's Letters, has a heavy focus on grace. The Greek word for "grace" (*charis*) occurs not at all in Matthew and Mark, only four times in John (all in the Prologue), and eight times in Luke (but not in the way Paul uses the term),[6] but it occurs seventeen times in Acts in theologically significant ways. Here, as with Paul's Letters, grace is an essential component of the gospel. In fact, the gospel can be summarized as the gospel of the grace of God (Acts 20:24), and while salvation comes through grace (15:11), grace is much more comprehensive and encompasses all of life, as several texts show.[7] In the next chapter we will see that Paul's use of grace language results from his encounter with the Greco-Roman world. Luke's use of the language seems to stem directly from Paul. In passing, we should note the two uses of the verb "justify" (*dikaioun*)

5. Acts 8:12; 19:8; 20:25; 28:23, 31.

6. In Luke, *charis* usually means "favor," as in Mary "found favor with God" (1:30). Perhaps Luke 4:22 is close to Paul's meaning. A few texts in Hebrews and 1 Peter also focus on grace.

7. See Acts 11:23; 13:43; 14:26; 18:27; and 20:32.

in a speech by Paul in Acts 13:38–39, which may reflect Paul's influence on Luke.

The Gospel of the End Time in Acts

While the kingdom and grace are important features in the presentation of the gospel in Acts, they are not really the focus. The central features of the gospel in Acts are the *death and resurrection of Jesus, his exaltation as Lord, and the giving of the Spirit*, all of which are still directly related to the kingdom and to the fulfillment of God's end-time promises.[8] *The Spirit is the very essence of Christianity*. It is no accident that Peter's Pentecost sermon starts with the pouring out of the Spirit and moves then to resurrection. In the Gospels the Spirit is the source of Jesus's identity. Jesus is the Messiah because he is anointed by the Spirit. The Spirit is also proof that the kingdom is already present in his ministry. In Acts the focus on the giving of the Spirit is enormous; it is viewed as the fulfillment of the Old Testament promises and as marking the beginning of the new age. The kingdom is present even more, and now the Spirit is the source of Christian identity. As with both John and Paul,[9] the Spirit is the source of conversion, and it is by the Spirit that Christians live. The gospel in the New Testament is a gospel about the Spirit.

At the beginning of this chapter, I asked what made the significance of Jesus's death and resurrection self-evident for Luke's

---

8. Summaries of the gospel may be found in Acts 2:17–36; 3:15, 19–20; 4:2, 10–12; 5:30–32; 10:36–44; 13:28–39; 16:31; 17:3, 18, 30–31; 19:4–6; 20:21; 22:14–16; 23:6; 24:15, 21, 25; 26:6–8, 18, 20, 22–23; and 28:23. Ben Meyer (*The Early Christians: Their World Mission and Self-Discovery* [Wilmington, DE: Michael Glazier, 1986], 19–20) argues that the salient elements of the early preaching were *reversal* (the stunning turn by which a slave's death was followed by enthronement as the Son of God), *anticipation* (the advance arrival of the end of history so that the Risen One offers the life of the age to come), and *convergence* (focusing fulfillment on a single person so that all the hopes of Israel and even Greece come to flower in him).

9. See esp. John 3:5–6; Rom. 5:5; and Gal. 3:2–3.

readers. They might ask us why it is not self-evident to us. Perhaps our familiarity with speaking of Jesus's death and resurrection makes them seem commonplace. Jesus's resurrection was a cataclysmic reversal of death. His resurrection was viewed not as a resuscitation but as the first resurrection of the general resurrection, the resurrection at the end of time (4:2; 26:23); therefore, *a shift in time has occurred*. God's end time has broken in, and Jesus's resurrection and pouring out of the Spirit are proof this is so. Peter's Pentecost sermon includes the quotation of Joel 2:28–32, but he adds the words "in the last days says God" to stress the point (Acts 2:17).[10] With this focus on the Spirit and resurrection, the gospel has to be seen as *eschatological*. If the gospel facts are true, if Jesus has been raised and has given the *end-time* Spirit, then Jesus is Lord, a truth that was then and is now the foundation for repentance and transformation.

The eschatological emphasis of the gospel comes through in other ways. Final judgment and the end-time coming of the Messiah are, at times, explicit themes in the preaching in Acts. Mostly, these ideas are more presupposed than stated, but they are important. Otherwise, the calls for repentance make no sense. Also, the expectation of future resurrection is presupposed, especially in Paul's assertion that he is on trial because of the hope of the resurrection (Acts 24:15).

Some texts, though, are explicit. In Acts 3:19–21 people are told, "Repent . . . so that times of refreshing may come from the presence of the Lord and that he may send the Messiah appointed for you, Jesus, whom heaven must receive until the time of the restoration of all things." In 17:31 Paul tells the Athenians that God has set a day on which the world will be judged in righteousness by the resurrected Christ. In 24:25 the topics of Paul's conversation with Felix are righteousness, self-control, and coming judgment.

10. See also Acts 14:16–17 and 17:30.

It is important to note that Acts—like Paul, John, and most of the New Testament—*never* mentions *gehenna* ("hell") or attempts to scare people into the kingdom.[11] Outside seven occurrences in Matthew and three in Mark, *gehenna* appears only at Luke 12:5 and James 3:6, the latter with reference to the tongue.[12] This takes nothing away from the seriousness of future judgment, but it does mark a gulf between how the gospel is presented in the New Testament and how it is often presented by some.

Acts does emphasize *salvation* language.[13] Salvation stems from God's grace, but the book does not allow any thought that, because of grace, humans do not act. People need to be saved from a perverse generation (Acts 2:40); consequently, repentance is an essential component of the gospel challenge and is emphasized in Acts as much as anywhere in the New Testament.[14]

Participation in Acts

But is participation with God or Christ present in Acts? Acts does not have Paul's emphasis on being in Christ or John's on remaining in Christ, but participation is very much the assumption of the whole book. Some texts do sound like Paul. Acts 17:28 records

11. The word "hades" in Acts 2:27, 31 refers merely to the realm of the dead, not hell. The closest Paul comes to speaking of hell is in 2 Thess. 1:7–8, which describes the revelation of the Lord from heaven in blazing fire giving vengeance.

12. The eleven occurrences in the Synoptic Gospels are all on the lips of Jesus. Revelation, in keeping with apocalyptic literature, does use "lake of fire." There are five occurrences. A few other terms occur in reference to judgment by fire, such as "furnace."

13. Twenty-two times, thirteen of which are the verb *sōzein*, six of which are the noun *sōtēria*, two of which are the noun *sōtēr*, and one of which is the noun *sōtērion*.

14. The noun *metanoia* ("repentance") appears in Acts 5:31; 11:18; 13:24; 19:4; 20:21; and 26:20. The last two are viewed as *positive* action, a turning to God and acting in ways worthy of repentance. The verb *metanoein* occurs in 2:38; 3:19; 8:22; 17:30; and 26:20. Another word meaning "repentance, a change in thinking"—*epistrophē*—appears in 15:3, and the corresponding verb *epistrephein*, "to repent," appears in 3:19; 9:35, 40; 11:21; 14:15; 15:19, 36; 16:18; 26:18, 20; and 28:27. The related word *apostrephein* ("to turn away") appears in 3:26.

Paul as saying, "God is the one *in whom* we live and move and are."[15] This is an extremely important text. It is not specifically about participation in Christ, but it points to something foundational and shows a presumption about what the relation between God and humans should be. God is the source and framework for all human existence. God is the context, the limit, the ground, and the motivation for all of life.

Several texts have the language of "believing into" that is so prevalent in John: Acts 10:43; 14:23; 19:4; 20:21; 24:24; and 26:18. We have already noted that *pisteuein eis* ("believe into") does not occur in secular Greek or in the Septuagint.[16] Why does this unusual language appear in Acts? Even if Acts means something less than John's "remaining in," the language still points to a participation with Christ that is much stronger than what the English "believe in" suggests. Further, people are encouraged to remain in God's grace (13:43) or are handed over to the grace of God by others. This sounds very much like Romans 5:2 ("this grace in which we stand") and grace as a sphere in which people live.[17] Clearly it shows an awareness of God's ongoing grace enabling life. Grace is not merely a factor at the entrance to faith; it is a power at work in the whole of Christian living.

By far the most obvious emphasis on participation in Acts is the interplay of God's action and human response. This huge theological topic frequently emerges in Scripture but is not explained. Acts witnesses over and over to the participation of God and humans together in whatever happens. God, Christ, and the Spirit all are involved, and so are humans.[18] People do not come into a

15. Conceivably, this should be translated "by whom," but even so, it would still emphasize a close interaction of God and humans. On this verse, see above p. 41, n. 11.

16. See p. 95.

17. First Corinthians 15:1 refers to the gospel in which (or on which) we stand.

18. This interplay of God's action and human response is evident elsewhere, not least in the double calling in Joel 2:32, part of which is quoted in Acts 2:21: "Then *everyone who calls on the name of the Lord* shall be saved; for in Mount Zion and in Jerusalem there shall be those who escape, as the Lord has said, and among the survivors shall be those *whom the Lord calls*." This last part of Joel

faith relation with God without God's acting or without their acting. People are exhorted to repent, but God gives repentance. We know the commands to repent, such as the one in Acts 2:38, "Repent and be baptized," but we forget texts like 3:26, which says God sent Christ "to bless you by turning each of you from your wicked ways," or 11:18, "Then even to the gentiles God has given repentance that leads to life."[19] People are urged to believe, but God enables belief. Acts 18:27 says Apollos was a great help to people in Achaia who *through grace* believed,[20] and 15:8–9 says the "heart-knowing" God cleansed the hearts of gentiles by faith. Acts 16:14 says God opened Lydia's heart to give heed to Paul's message. People are to seek God (17:27) at the same time God is seeking them. The "builders" (Jewish leaders) rejected Jesus, but all was ordained by God's hand (4:11 and 28). God sent to Peter the people Cornelius sent to Peter (10:8 and 20). God gives healing, but people give evidence of the possibility of healing, for 14:9 says Paul recognized that a man had faith to be healed. The stance people have is crucial. Are they open, willing to hear and obey, or are their hearts hardened and already closed? As in John 7:17, the willingness to obey is key to discerning and receiving the message.[21] If you are not willing to obey, you will find an excuse not to believe. From all this it is obvious that the human response to God already involves the participation of God. God is the primary actor in the book of Acts—and in all of life.

The relation between human responsibility and God's initiative is unresolved in Acts, which creates difficulty for us, but I doubt early Christians even saw the problem. The tension we feel results from the incorrect assumption that God is distant and waiting for us to come to him. People were never intended to be separate from

---

2:32 (Hebrew 3:5) is brought back in at Acts 2:39. See also Jer. 31:18–19; Lam. 5:21; and John 6:44, 47.

19. See also Acts 3:19 and 5:31.

20. See also Acts 13:48; 14:27; and 15:7.

21. See Klyne Snodgrass, "Reading to Hear: A Hermeneutics of Hearing," *Horizons in Biblical Theology* 24 (2002): 1–32, esp. 28–29.

God. Whether or not one knows it or likes it, to be human is to be engaged with God. *Participation is the key to understanding the relation between divine sovereignty and human freedom.* God works in us, and we choose to respond. Without our response God's work is not accomplished. It is not that God is limited by us; rather, God chooses not to overpower. God seeks relation, and relation is a two-way street. It cannot legitimately be forced. Consequently, salvation is totally the work of God in which we are totally involved. It could be no other way. Luke knows that salvation involves both being grasped by God and grasping onto what God has done in Christ. Paul says essentially the same thing in Philippians 3:12: "I press on, if indeed I may take hold of that for which I was taken hold of by Christ." Salvation is involvement with God that, by grace, reorients life and makes one a participant in the kingdom and a follower of Jesus.

The other key and obvious part of the gospel in Acts is the transformation and godly living that results. No passivity is suggested or allowed, nor is any thought that conversion is some type of individualistic affair. The result of the Spirit coming at Pentecost shows that conversion brings people into a believing, learning, worshiping community that shares with those in need—radically so in their selling resources to assist those in need. The transformation in how money is viewed is evident in nearly every chapter of Acts. People are expected to live out their repentance in a way that shows it is genuine—"doing works worthy of repentance" (26:20). In 6:7 many priests *obey* with respect to the faith, reminding us of "the obedience of faith" in Romans 1:5 and 16:26. Early Christians never had any difficulty linking obedience and faith. They would have thought it odd not to do so. Acts may spend relatively little time offering explicit ethical teaching, but it still stresses that the ethical implications of life with Christ are enormous.

Acts does not betray much of Paul's or John's ideas of living in Christ, but it reveals intriguing parallels to both. Still, the gospel in Acts is a gospel of participation, first of all in the appropriation of the gospel. In the introduction, one of my initial questions about the gospel was this: how is the gospel appropriated? The answer of the book of Acts is that God enables the appropriation, giving repentance, granting grace to believe, and endowing with the Spirit, the source of all good things—but not without the person acting to appropriate the gospel by repenting, trusting, receiving the Spirit willingly, and obeying. The role of the Spirit is central.

Acts directly addresses most of the other questions from the introduction. Why does anyone need the gospel? Because of sins, darkness, and ignorance. What is the gospel? It is God's long story with Israel about God's care and involvement, which comes to a climax in the death and resurrection of Jesus and the giving of the Spirit. What specifically do the death and resurrection of Jesus have to do with the gospel? They are the gospel. Acts does not explain why the death and resurrection are so much the focus, but these events are seen as the fulfillment of the Scriptures, the beginning of the end time, the promise of future resurrection, and the fountain for the forgiveness of sins. If the promises are fulfilled about God being king and the Spirit being poured out to transform lives, this is good news worth sharing. To what degree is the gospel eschatological? Completely, because of the breaking in of the end in the resurrection and pouring out of the Spirit, because of judgment, and because of future life with God. How should the gospel be articulated? That is up to us. Acts can insist on the character of the gospel, but how the gospel should be expressed in our time is a question we will have to answer, with no lessening of the central features of the message as Acts presents it: death and resurrection, Spirit, engagement with God, forgiveness, salvation, peace, moral transformation, and expectation of judgment and ongoing life with God.

eight

Paul's Letters: *How Does Salvation Work, and for What Purpose?*

For the average person, Christianity has shriveled to sheer mean-inglessness, a burlesque edition of the doctrine of grace, that if one is a Christian one lets things go their way and counts on God's grace. . . .

Nothing can be taken in vain as easily as grace; as soon as imitation [of Christ] is completely omitted, grace is taken in vain. But that is the kind of preaching people like.

Søren Kierkegaard[1]

I grew up in the mountains of east Tennessee, and I love mountains. Pictures of mountains are impressive and enjoyable, but looking at a picture is nothing compared to being in the mountains or on the top of a mountain. This experience of being there is what the

1. Søren Kierkegaard, *Søren Kierkegaard's Journals and Papers*, trans. Howard V. Hong and Edna H. Hong (Bloomington: Indiana University Press, 1970), 2:1878, quoted in the supplement to Kierkegaard, *Practice in Christianity*, ed. and trans. Howard V. Hong and Edna H. Hong, Kierkegaard's Writings 20 (Princeton: Princeton University Press, 1991), 352–53.

gospel of participation is about, and where you do things matters. Singing in the shower is not like singing in Carnegie Hall. What will enable us to know that our new geography of being in Christ matters to such an extent that we experience "being there"?

In our time the focus of the gospel is debated, with some scholars severely criticizing others if they do not use the exact right words or have just the right emphasis. This is especially true of those who think justification language or penal substitution are the "real" ways to speak of salvation. Justification and substitution are crucial concepts, but they are open to misunderstanding and do not provide all we need in explaining the gospel. Participation is much more comprehensive and helpful.

If participation is so great, how does it really help us understand our relation with God and what Christ has accomplished for us? What difference does it make when we think of salvation and how atonement works? How does it change what we say about ethics and ministry? To address these questions, I return to Paul's Letters, for they, as much as anywhere, provide answers to crucial questions about appropriating the gospel and expressing it.

In the introduction I listed six questions crucial to my course on the gospel. The most difficult for many people to grasp and answer is the question, "How is the gospel appropriated?" What is it that makes Jesus's death of any benefit for people living almost two thousand years later? Further, what does this remote death have to do with our lives today? If his death is merely a tragedy or even a nice example of courage, who cares? We have millions of such examples. But Christ's death is not some remote event. *The gospel is that his death is your death and his life is your life.* That may sound strange, but it is a pretty good exchange[2]—and it is the gospel.

---

2. Or as John Calvin puts it, "This is the wonderful exchange which, out of his measureless benevolence, he has made with us." Calvin, *Institutes of the Christian Religion*, trans. Ford Lewis Battles, 2 vols., Library of Christian Classics 20 (Philadelphia: Westminster, 1960), 4.17.2. Think, too, of Matt. 16:24–26/Mark 8:34–36/ Luke 9:23–25.

An African American spiritual, apparently composed by slaves, asks, "Were you there when they crucified my Lord?" The question seems silly; of course we were not there, chronologically and geographically. But the question in the song is not silly. These slaves identified with the suffering of Christ and saw their experience mirrored in his. The New Testament message is that if you are a Christian, you were indeed there—in Christ. His death is your death, and his life is your life.

This involvement in Christ's death and life is what the gospel of participation asserts and offers, and there is *no other* Christian gospel. Participation provides a huge advantage in explaining how the gospel is appropriated and what it has to do with us, especially in providing a foundation for ethics. Participation taken seriously is helpful in addressing several theological questions, but it is absolutely essential for understanding salvation and ethics. There is good reason that being in Christ is the dominant motif in Paul's thought, and without a focus on participation there is no chance of understanding Paul—or the Christian faith.

I have pointed to the different ways the gospel is presented with different New Testament authors. They all focus on Jesus's death and resurrection and being bound to him, but they express the gospel with different language and images. Paul's Letters themselves vary *considerably* in the way the gospel is described. The Greek verb *dikaioun* ("to justify"), which is so important in Romans and Galatians, appears only four times in all the other letters.[3] The noun *sōma* ("body"), which dominates 1 Corinthians, Ephesians, and Colossians and is important in Romans, occurs only once in Galatians and once in 1 Thessalonians, and in neither case does it have the theological significance it does elsewhere. There is no value in trying to level out the differences.

We should remind ourselves that in none of the letters is Paul simply defining the gospel. He is *applying* the gospel to the

3. First Corinthians 4:4; 6:11; 1 Tim. 3:16; and Titus 3:7.

circumstances and problems of the recipients. Even in Romans, where Paul is laying out his gospel in hopes of support for his mission to Spain, he is addressing, at least partly, issues in the Roman church concerning the relation of Jews and gentiles, which is indeed at the heart of his gospel. One thing is clear, though: in all the letters the "in Christ" thinking and ideas of participation with the risen Christ are evident, frequent, and foundational.

Another fact must be faced. People today may identify as Christians because of the compelling and attractive teaching of Jesus, and justly so. However, outside the Gospels, most of the New Testament does not give much explicit attention to the teaching of Jesus. The writers focus on Jesus's death and resurrection. No doubt, as the Gospels themselves attest, early Christians savored Jesus's teaching, and allusions to his teaching are often evident.[4] Most importantly, Jesus's discipleship teaching on denying self, taking a cross, and following have the same intent as the church's teaching on identification with Jesus's death and resurrection. The focus of the Christian faith is on participation with the death and resurrection of Christ, not just on his teaching, although conformity to that teaching is a natural consequence. Faith is attachment to and discipleship to a crucified and risen Lord.

In my commentary on Ephesians I argue that Christology is soteriology is ecclesiology is ethics.[5] That is not good grammar, but it is good theology. What you believe about Jesus Christ will determine what you believe about salvation, and what you conclude about salvation will determine your understanding of the church, which will determine also your understanding of how you should and must live. In this chapter I will not treat the person and work of Christ or the nature of the church, but I will treat two of the most important texts describing salvation: 2 Corinthians

4. Not least in Rom. 12–15. See Michael Thompson, *Clothed with Christ: The Example and Teaching of Jesus in Romans 12:1–15:13* (Sheffield: JSOT Press, 1991). There are also frequent allusions in the book of James.

5. Klyne Snodgrass, *Ephesians*, NIV Application Commentary (Grand Rapids: Zondervan, 1996), 146.

5:14–6:4 and Ephesians 2:4–10. In these two the focus is more on salvation, but ethics is very much present. In the next chapter I will treat two other crucial texts—Romans 6:1–14 and 1 Corinthians 6:12–20—where the concern is more on ethics but salvation is still front and center.

This is not to suggest we could treat texts regarding salvation and then treat texts on ethics. That cannot be done. All the texts, and not just the four texts chosen, encompass both. Neither Paul nor any other New Testament writer separates salvation and ethics. To be saved by Jesus is to be given over to the ethic of Jesus.

In selecting these four texts, I feel guilty for not treating other crucial texts. *All* of Paul's Letters focus on participation. To assuage my guilt, let me challenge readers to read Philippians with a participation lens. Participation with God and Christ by the Spirit and with others in the body of Christ is the basis of the whole letter, even though *sōma* ("body") appears only three times, none with the theological significance of the other letters.

How Does Salvation Work Anyway?

People often view Jesus as our substitute and our representative, and both are true, but both strike many people as odd, artificial, and foreign. We did not choose him as our substitute and did not vote for him as our representative. Substitution suggests that Jesus takes our place and we are no longer on the scene, which is just wrong. The whole idea of a representative falls short. Most of us do not know our representatives in government, are not close to them, and do not feel close to them, so why should we, how can we, feel close to Jesus? Both substitution and representation are valid ideas, but they fail to do justice to the New Testament teaching. "His death is your death, and his life is your life" is about far more than substitution or representation, as all four texts will show.

2 Corinthians 5:14–6:4

14 For Christ's love compels us, for we have concluded this: one died for [on behalf of] all; therefore, all died. 15 He died for all so that the ones living no longer live for themselves but for the one who died for them and was raised. 16 As a result, from now on, we know no one in a merely human way. Even if once we knew Christ in a merely human way, we do not know him that way now. 17 So then, if anyone is in Christ, new creation has occurred! Old things have passed away; new things have come into being. 18 All these things are from God, who reconciled us to himself through Christ and gave us the ministry of reconciliation. 19 God was in Christ reconciling the world to himself, not counting people's sins against them and entrusting us with the message of reconciliation. 20 Therefore, we are ambassadors on behalf of Christ; God is making his appeal through us. We implore you on behalf of Christ: be reconciled to God. 21 God made the one who knew no sin to be sin for us that we might become the righteousness of God in him.

6:1 We are working together with God and urge you not to receive the grace of God to no effect. 2 For Scripture says, "At a favorable time I heard you, and in the day of salvation I helped you" [Isa. 49:8]. Now is the favorable time. Now is the day of salvation. 3 We give no cause of offense to anyone so that our ministry is not discredited, 4 but in everything we commend ourselves as servants of God with much endurance, in afflictions, in calamities, in difficulties . . .

This text is part of a long discourse about ministry that extends from 2:14 to 7:4. It emphasizes the character, motives, and difficulties of Paul's work, and his overriding motive is the reconciling love of Christ and God. This is one of the most descriptive, nuanced, and powerful texts on salvation in the New Testament.[6] The first thing one encounters is the love of Christ and "One died for all;

6. For a longer treatment of this text, see Klyne Snodgrass, "Reconciliation—God Being God with Special Reference to 2 Corinthians 5:11–6:4," *Covenant Quarterly* 60, no. 2 (May 2002): 3–23.

therefore, all died," which is a stunning statement. This goes well beyond substitution and representation; it is participation and involvement. How can it be that all died when Christ died? Verse 14 focuses on Christ's love for humanity and *his* participation with us. The purpose of the incarnation is for Christ to participate with humanity, identify with and become one with humanity, take on humanity's burden of sin, and give himself for humanity.

The verses that follow provide commentary on verse 14 and show the result of Christ's love and action, and it is all about participation. The commentary comes especially in verses 18–19 and 21. In verses 18–19 we are told that all the new creation and transformation described in verses 14–17 comes from God, who reconciled us to himself through Christ, and that "God was in Christ reconciling the world to himself, not counting people's sins against them." It is worth remembering that only Paul uses reconciliation language[7] and that God is always the one who reconciles and is never said to be reconciled.[8] God does not need to be reconciled. *God is for us*, always moving toward us, and God does the reconciling, even when the wrath of God because of sin is a reality not to be downplayed. It is not that Christ loves us and reconciles us to God. No, God is the one who reconciles through Christ. The initiative is entirely God's and is independent of us.

---

7. The verb *katallassein* appears only in Rom. 5:10 (2x); 1 Cor. 7:11 (with regard to marriage); and 2 Cor. 5:18, 19, 20. The noun *katallagē* appears only in Rom. 5:11; 11:15; and 2 Cor. 5:18, 19. The verb *apokatallassein*, which appears to be a new word coined by Paul, occurs only in Eph. 2:16 and Col. 1:20, 22. Cognates do appear in other New Testament writings. *Allassein*, which means "to change" or "to exchange," occurs in Acts 6:14; Rom. 1:23; 1 Cor. 15:51, 52; Gal. 4:20; and Heb. 1:12. *Metallassein* is parallel to *allassein* in Rom. 1:25, 26. *Synallassein* (Acts 7:26), *diallassesthai* (Matt. 5:24), and *apallassein* (Luke 12:58) are used of the restoration of human relations. Hebrews 2:15 uses *apallassein* to describe release from the tyranny of the fear of death, and Acts 19:12 uses it to describe healing from disease. *Antallagma* and *parallagē* both retain the nuance of change or exchange. The former occurs only in Matt. 16:26/Mark 8:37 ("What will a person give in *exchange* for his or her life?"). The latter occurs only in James 1:17 to say there is no variation in God at all.

8. If the verb is active, God is the subject. If the verb is passive, humans are the subject.

While reconciliation language in the New Testament appears only in Romans, 2 Corinthians, Ephesians, and Colossians,[9] it is in many ways the most useful language for describing what happens with the gospel. People may be unsure what to do with words like "justification" and "redemption," but "reconciliation" is common language, is easily understood, focuses on relationships, and is the least metaphorical of all the salvation terms. It is the most needed and practical language for our fractured world, for it summarizes the notion of peace that is at the heart of the gospel—peace with God instead of wrath, peace made possible for divided groups, and peace within ourselves.

Reconciliation encapsulates several crucial ideas, including enmity caused by sin, sins not being taken into account, and unity with Christ. We can understand why Peter Stuhlmacher describes reconciliation as the heartbeat and the main theme of the New Testament[10] and why Ralph Martin says reconciliation is the interpretive key to the whole of Paul's theology and the center of his missionary and pastoral work.[11] Obviously, too, reconciliation is through and through about participation.

The statement "God was *in* Christ reconciling" could be taken as a reference to the incarnation or could mean God, *by means of* Christ, was reconciling. Probably the latter is intended, but likely neither Paul nor his Greek readers thought about the difference. God was making a move to restore humanity to himself, and his act of participation via Christ's life, death, and resurrection was the means of doing so. Our focus must be heavily *on God moving to bring people back to himself. God will have a people.* No other avenue of return exists. Christ is the revelation of God as

9. That is, the words *katallassein*, *katallagē*, and *apokatallassein*, the words used for salvation.

10. Peter Stuhlmacher, "The Gospel of Reconciliation in Christ: Basic Features and Issues of a Biblical Theology of the New Testament," *Horizons in Biblical Theology* 1 (1979): 161–90, esp. 180–85.

11. Ralph P. Martin, *Reconciliation: A Study of Paul's Theology* (Atlanta: John Knox, 1981), 5.

the God who gives himself, even in the context of his wrath, and reconciles. Revelation and reconciliation are the very character of God's being, but Christ is just as much the revelation of what true humanity is. The first and determinative aspect of participation is God's participation with humanity via Christ. This is to say God did something concrete and specific for humanity through the life, death, and resurrection of Christ, and the emphasis falls on what happened at Golgotha and the empty tomb. God took the initiative in order to avoid taking our sins into account.

God's participation with us through Christ creates a solidarity with us. This assumption is the reason for Paul's emphasis on the image of the body of Christ, possibly the most important metaphor in all his letters. We are *part of Christ*, and as a result of being in him, we are *part of those in Christ*.[12] What happens to Christ involves us, and what happens to us involves Christ. The depth to which Paul understood this is evident in 1 Corinthians 8:12: "Thus when you sin against brothers and sisters and strike their weak conscience, you sin against Christ." This mirrors Jesus's statement in Matthew 25:40: "Whatever you did to one of these least brothers and sisters of mine, you did to me." This solidarity created by God enables both salvation and life.

Does "one died, therefore all died" imply universalism? Not in the sense that all are saved, even if they do not know it, or will be in the end. Verse 14 describes only the first half of participation, as the rest of the passage makes clear. The *extent* of verse 14 is universal,[13] but it does *not* lead to universalism, for human response is required in identification with Christ's dying and rising. We will consider the human response shortly, but clearly this passage—at least to me—excludes any idea of limited atonement, the idea that Christ's death was effective only for the elect.

12. See pp. 38 and 45.
13. I do not think the attempt to limit "all" to "all believers" has any basis, and it sounds like special pleading.

Christ's death is potentially effective for all, but not without their involvement.

Verse 21 provides further commentary and is a crucial text on participation: "God made the one who knew no sin to be sin for us that we might become the righteousness of God in him." The intent of this tightly wound summary is debated. People often emphasize substitution or "imputation," the latter meaning that God imputed (ascribed or attributed) righteousness—Christ's righteousness, an "alien" righteousness—to us. Certainly, any righteousness accorded us is "alien" in that it is totally from Christ and is not our own, but substitution and imputation, as important as they are, can be misleading and do not communicate well.[14]

Substitution rightly sees Christ as taking our place, but it removes us from the picture. Imputation suggests something akin to inoculation and is hardly biblical language. Surely, too, most people's eyes glaze over with such language, and the discussions feel like putting on Saul's armor. The text is much more about *participation*. God made the one without sin, Jesus Christ, a participant with sinful humanity that *in him* they might participate in his righteousness. This exchange, or interchange,[15] between Christ and humanity is what the gospel, the gospel of participation, is about. This benefit of righteousness takes place only because he participated with us and we participate with him to such an extent

14. See James D. G. Dunn, *The Theology of Paul the Apostle* (Grand Rapids: Eerdmans, 1998), 223: "Substitution tells only half the story. There is . . . an important element of Jesus taking the place of others—that, after all, is at the heart of the sacrificial metaphor. But Paul's teaching is *not* that Christ dies 'in the place of' others so that they *escape* death (as the logic of 'substitution' implies). It is rather that Christ's sharing *their* death makes it possible for them to share *his* death" (italics original).

15. Morna Hooker has four very helpful articles on salvation as interchange. See "Interchange in Christ," *Journal of Theological Studies* 22 (1971): 349–61; "Interchange and Atonement," *Bulletin of the John Rylands Library* 60 (1978): 462–81; "Interchange and Suffering," in *Suffering and Martyrdom in the New Testament*, ed. William Horbury and Brian McNeill (Cambridge: Cambridge University Press, 1981), 70–83; and "Interchange in Christ and Ethics," *Journal for the Study of the New Testament* 25 (1985): 3–17.

that we are *in him*, have solidarity with him, and are joined to him to take on his character. The only cases in which God considers people to be just are when there is attachment to Christ, never when one is viewed by himself or herself alone. One is just by being bound to the covenant-making God, just as Abraham was. Much of what is in 5:21 seems to be drawn directly from the suffering servant language in Isaiah 52:13–53:12. In Christ, God took on the iniquity of us all (53:6) and set it aside. His death is our death, and his life is our life.

The other side of participation, the human side, is just as strong in this passage. How could it not be if we have been compelled by Christ's love, as verse 14 says? People are urged to be reconciled to God and not to receive the grace of God to no effect (5:20 and 6:1). In other words, do not allow this gospel to be useless and without results in your life. To be reconciled is to become a reconciling agent. Christians identify with Christ and participate with Christ to such an extent that they are said to be *in him* (vv. 17 and 21).[16] They become the righteousness of God *in him* (v. 21). They become marked by his righteousness. *Christ's purpose in identifying with humanity is ethical transformation.* People in Christ no longer live an isolated life to themselves; they live for the crucified and risen Lord, who chose participation with them (v. 15). Salvation and ethics are a piece of the same cloth.

A present eschatological perspective marks the text as a result of the resurrection. That is only to say that the benefits expected at the end of time are already at work, even if they are not complete. *Now* no one is viewed from a merely human point of view. Implied is that people are viewed from the perspective of what God is doing in Christ. Old things have passed away; new creation has broken in (5:16–17). *Now* is the time of salvation (6:2).

16. Second Corinthians 5:17 is blunter than most translations show. A more literal translation would be, "So then, if anyone is in Christ, new creation! Old things have passed; see, new things have come." The KJV's "*all* things are become new" derives from an addition to the manuscript tradition and has little claim to being original.

Believers are given the task and privilege of participating in God's ministry of reconciling (5:18). They are said to be *partners/co-workers* with God, working together with God (6:1)[17] and being servants of God (6:4). They become reconciling agents like their Lord.

In 5:20 Paul says that "we," on behalf of Christ, as ambassadors of Christ and with God urging through us, implore people to be reconciled to God. This is no mild engagement with God and God's work. Whether with the first-person-plural pronouns Paul thinks only of himself and Timothy or has in mind the task of all Christians is debated. Even if the focus is on Paul and Timothy because of tensions with the Corinthians, the passage transcends the Corinthian context and speaks of salvation more generally. In the end what is said applies to all believers. Paul has a high view of his own apostolic office, but he has no thought that participation in the task of God, working together with God, is limited to only a few "apostolic" folk. Too many other people are designated as co-workers or described as laboring in or for the Lord, language Paul uses of himself.[18]

Participation is still the theme in 6:14–18, only this time the focus is on excluding the wrong kind of participation, participation with unbelief, sin, and idolatry. Six different terms underscore the focus on participation: "yoked with something that is a mismatch," "partnership," "joint sharing," "in common with," "harmony," and "agreement."[19] In contrast to such inappropriate

---

17. Some try to resist the idea of working together with God, but what else does *synergountes* ("working together with") in 6:1 entail, esp. after "as God is making his appeal through us" in 5:20? See also 1 Cor. 3:9 and 1 Thess. 3:2.

18. *Synergos*, "fellow worker," is used of Paul (1 Cor. 3:9), Priscilla and Aquila (Rom. 16:3), Urbanus (Rom. 16:9), Timothy (Rom. 16:21 and 1 Thess. 3:2), the Corinthians in general (2 Cor. 1:24), Titus (2 Cor. 8:23), Epaphroditus (Phil. 2:25), Euodia and Syntyche (Phil. 4:3), Justus (Col. 4:11), Philemon (Philem. 1), and Mark, Aristarchus, Demas, and Luke (Philem. 24). The verb *kopian* ("to labor") is used of Paul's own ministry (1 Cor. 15:10 and several others), of four women (Rom. 16:6, 12), of leaders generally (1 Cor. 16:16 and 1 Thess. 5:12), and of teaching elders (1 Tim. 5:17).

19. *Heterozygein, metochē, koinōnia, symphōnēsis, meris,* and *synkatathesis*.

participation, believers are described as a temple of God, and God will dwell with them, walk about with them, welcome them, and be their God and Father. This is all strong participation language.

So how does salvation work? Without oversimplifying atonement ideas, salvation works by participation. Salvation is conveyed and appropriated because God in Christ loves and participates with the human race; takes their burden of sins and does not count their sins, *because of the cross*; takes people into his own being; and reconciles them to himself. *God makes salvation work.* Humans participate by responding to God's love and forgiveness, acknowledging their dying with Christ ("for we have concluded this" in 5:14) and no longer living to themselves but participating in the life and work God gives. To what end is salvation? Nothing less than life with God and engagement in the work of God. All is based on union with God and Christ that transforms life. Without such participation and union, salvation cannot happen.

Ephesians 2:4-10

[4] But God, being rich in mercy, because of his great love with which he loved us, [5] and although we were dead because of sins, made us alive with Christ—by grace you are saved—[6] and he raised us with him and seated us with him in the heavenly regions in Christ Jesus. [7] He did this to demonstrate in the coming ages the extraordinary wealth of his grace shown in his kindness to us in Christ Jesus. [8] For by grace you are saved through faith, and this salvation is not from you. It is the gift of God [9] and not something attained from works, so that no one can boast. [10] We are the result of God's work, created in Christ Jesus to do good works that God prepared ahead of time that we should live [walk] in them.

Ephesians has as much focus on participation as any part of Scripture. As mentioned earlier, the six chapters of this letter have "in Christ" language or its equivalent (like "in him," "in the Lord," or "in whom") thirty-six times, twenty-three of which are in chapters 1 and 2, and eleven of those are in 1:3–14. All of God's work is encapsulated in Christ. Even election takes place in Christ, for people are elect in the elect One (1:4).[20] In addition, Ephesians has fourteen "with" compounds such as one finds in 3:6: "so that the gentiles might be *heirs with* and *body with* and *partakers with* the promises in Christ Jesus through the gospel." Ephesians also emphasizes corporate images like the body, the temple, and the new being.[21] In 5:30 Christians are said to be members of Christ's body, part of Christ, and in 4:25 to be members of each other, part of each other. Paul takes seriously the body metaphor as expressing solidarity with both Christ and fellow believers—a thoroughgoing participation in both directions. Because of this, divisions of race, gender, and ethnicity are set aside. If you are part of other believers, valuations based on such claims of status make no sense. All racism is excluded—period. In 2:19–22 Christians are part of the family of God, a building joined together in Christ and growing into a temple in which God dwells by his Spirit. Such images exclude any thought of distance from God or a mild relation to God, as well as any thought of disdain for other believers—or for anyone.

With all this focus on being in and with Christ, it is no surprise to find participation at the heart of Ephesians 2:4–10. This passage provides one of the most powerful summaries of Paul's gospel, and it is a gospel of participation with Christ. As in 2 Corinthians 5:14–6:4, *God* dominates the text, and the focus is on God's participation with humans. Again the motivation of God's act is his great love. *God is for us.* God made believers alive with Christ, raised them with Christ, and seated them with Christ in the heavenly realms, three examples of "with" compounds (vv. 5 and 6). Here the focus is not on dying with Christ but on resurrection with Christ. The death imagery shifts to focus instead on the human deadness caused by sin, but the cross is still very much the basis of salvation, as 1:7; 2:13–16; and 5:2 and 25 attest.

---

20. See the discussion of election in Snodgrass, *Ephesians*, 48–50, 57–59, 64–65.
21. The new being in 2:15 is corporate, whereas in 4:24 it is individual.

All this activity of God comes as a sheer gift (v. 8), which is underscored by the repetition of the word "grace," and the location of this work of God is "in Christ Jesus," a fact that is emphasized three times in these six verses (vv. 6, 7, 10).

Paul was *the* theologian of grace, and he knew *grace was a power* that put him to work (1 Cor. 15:10). His use of "grace" language resulted especially from his encounter with the Greco-Roman patronage system, where "grace" was used to describe the benefits a patron bestowed on "worthy" recipients, who in turn would then bestow honor to the patron by showing gratitude and being indebted to the patron. It assumed a system of reciprocity and often was a show of pride, especially by the emperors.[22] The grace of the gospel is quite different. God's grace is given to *unworthy* recipients, and his giving is grounded only in his own character. Grace does not come without obligation, however. To receive grace is to be both obligated to and empowered by the Giver.

People would like to have the gift of salvation without its responsibilities, but that is impossible. You cannot have the gift apart from the Giver—apart from participation with the Giver. Grace is nothing other than God giving us himself. The gift is the Giver, as people like Søren Kierkegaard, Ernst Käsemann,[23] and others have asserted, and the Giver by necessity changes your life. We know the gospel is described as the power of God in Romans 1:16 and 1 Corinthians 1:18. Did you think you could encounter the power of God and it would leave you unscathed? If you were not changed, you did not get it.

22. See James R. Harrison, *Paul's Language of Grace in Its Graeco-Roman Context*, Wissenschaftliche Untersuchungen zum Neuen Testament 2/172 (Tübingen: Mohr Siebeck, 2003).

23. Kierkegaard, *Practice in Christianity*, 39; Ernst Käsemann, "Ministry and Community in the New Testament," *Essays on New Testament Themes* (Philadelphia: Fortress, 1964), 63–94, here 65, 74–75; and Käsemann, "'The Righteousness of God' in Paul," in *New Testament Questions of Today*, trans. W. J. Montague (London: SCM, 1969), 168–82, here 170, 174.

Such change is presumed in the description of believers as seated in the heavenly realms *in Christ Jesus* (Eph. 2:6). This is primarily a way to say their true identity—and therefore their actions—is determined by the risen Christ. Future life with God is important, for the wealth of God's grace will be demonstrated in the coming ages *in Christ Jesus* (2:7), but the focus is on the present and the fact that believers are the result of God's work, created *in Christ Jesus* to walk/live in the good works God prepared for them to do (2:10). As in the Old Testament, in the rest of the letter, "walk," often translated as "live," is a key word to describe living in relation to God. All the benefits of God's work—past, present, and future—are to be found in Christ Jesus, and life is summed up as a walk with him. As before, the text is about God's creating a framework for participation. In Christ, God creates a solidarity with humans and participates with them, but God also enables humans to be in solidarity with Christ and participate with him.

The human aspect of participation is less in focus, but it is obviously present at two points: faith in verse 8[24] and, in verse 10, the good works in which we are to live. Faith is not the gift of God; rather, the whole salvation enterprise is the gift of God. Still, we should not think human believing, as important as it is, places us in Christ. Being placed in Christ is itself the work of God. As verse 9 points out, nothing about salvation can legitimately be seen as a human accomplishment about which one can boast. As we saw with the book of Acts, even our response to God is a participation with God. Even so, texts like this one should have prevented the isolation of faith from works and the illegitimate and misleading faith-works discussion. Faith works, or it is not faith.

The passages that follow likewise stress ideas of participation, being in Christ, and the consequences. "In Christ" and related expressions and "in the Spirit" appear eleven times in Ephesians 2:11–22. *Now* people previously excluded are brought near (2:13).

---

24. Assuming the reference is to human faith and not to the faithfulness of God.

Barriers between God and humans and between people groups are broken down, because Christ is our peace. Racism cannot be true of those in Christ. The divided groups (specifically Jews and gentiles) are together reconciled to God in one body (2:14–16). This passage on reconciliation expands the themes we saw in 2 Corinthians 5:14–6:4. As there, the death of Christ is emphasized, but much of the focus here is on living with God (Eph. 2:18–20).

From such assumptions of union with Christ and a new identity in Christ, Paul, the prisoner *in the Lord*, urges people to live (literally "walk") worthy of the calling with which they were called (Eph. 4:1). The rest of the letter spells out the demands of such a statement. In short, participation with Christ will result in praise, humility, unity, living the truth in love, building up the body of Christ, mutual submission, and refusal to participate with evil.[25]

How does salvation work? By participation—God's participation with us and ours with God. Because of this solidarity, what happened in Jesus's death and resurrection did not happen merely to him. It included believers. Faith enables a solidarity with Christ so that what happened to him happened to them. Believers were indeed there at the cross. For what purpose is salvation given? Here, as elsewhere, there is no mention of going to heaven, even as a future with God is anticipated. The "heavenly places" are mentioned to assert that your identity in Christ is not of human origin. Your identity is derived from a different geography, the heavenly realms, where God is. The goal is productive living with God and as God intended. Again salvation and ethics are inseparable.

---

25. See esp. 3:21; 4:2–3, 15–16; 5:18–21; and 5:3–12, respectively.

nine

Paul's Letters: How Does Salvation Work, and *for What Purpose?*

But if there is only one rescue for us, Christianity, then there truly is only one possible rescue for Christianity: rigorousness.

Søren Kierkegaard[1]

In his writings Søren Kierkegaard often emphasized both the words "rigorousness" and "earnestness" to convince people to take Christianity seriously. It is odd, isn't it, that one has to plea for people to take Christianity seriously, when everything involved has to do with God and the seriousness of life?

I have a friend who is a helicopter mechanic. Obviously, his job is important, and he must do it seriously with rigorousness and earnestness. Just how rigorous he must be is revealed in a requirement of his job: after his repairs he has to be on board the next flight of the helicopter. He does his work earnestly and

1. Søren Kierkegaard, *Practice in Christianity*, ed. and trans. Howard V. Hong and Edna H. Hong, Kierkegaard's Writings 20 (Princeton: Princeton University Press, 1991), 227–28.

seriously! But all of life is important. Why do people, especially people claiming faith, not live with such focus and care?

Salvation works because of participation with Christ, and its purpose is moral transformation. Christ may have died for the ungodly, but not so they could stay ungodly; rather, he died that they may be transformed and become godly, characterized by their God. This is the argument of the two passages treated in this chapter— Romans 6:1–14 and 1 Corinthians 6:12–20. Both passages emphasize the transformation that participation enables and demands.

If, as Paul says in Romans 5:20–21, grace overflows where sin multiplies, wouldn't more sin produce more grace? This silly reasoning, which is the question he raises in 6:1, appears because Paul had apparently been accused of being morally lax. No doubt the accusation resulted from what he said about freedom and the law. Romans 3:8 already mentioned this charge: "Some say we say, 'Let's do bad things that good things may come,'" an accusation he rejects hands down, but now in chapter 6 he returns to a lengthier treatment and insists on moral transformation.

Romans 6:1–14[2]

[1] What say we say, then? Shall we continue with sin that grace might increase? [2] No way! How can those of us who died to sin still live in it? [3] Or are you unaware that we who were baptized into Christ Jesus were baptized into his death? [4] We were buried with him through baptism into death so that just as Christ was raised from the dead through the glory of the Father, so we also should live [literally "walk"] in newness of life. [5] For if we have been united to a death like his, indeed we will be united to a resurrection like his. [6] We know that our old being was crucified with him that the

2. For a broader treatment of this text, see Klyne Snodgrass, "Baptized into Christ: Romans 6:3–4—*The* Text on Baptism and Participation," in *Cruciform Scripture: Cross, Participation, and Mission; Essays in Honor of Michael J. Gorman*, ed. Christopher W. Skinner, Nijay K. Gupta, Andy Johnson, and Drew J. Strait (Grand Rapids: Eerdmans, 2020), 106–22.

body of sin might be nullified, so that we no longer serve sin. [7] For the one who died has been acquitted [justified] from sin. [8] If we died with Christ, we believe that also we will live with him, [9] and we know that since Christ has been raised from the dead, he no longer dies. Death is no longer lord over him. [10] For the death he died, he died to sin once for all. The life he lives, he lives to God. [11] So, you consider yourselves dead to sin but living to God in Christ Jesus. [12] Therefore, do not let sin rule your mortal body so that you obey its desires, [13] and do not present any part of yourself to sin as an instrument for wrongdoing. Rather, present yourselves to God as brought to life from the dead and every part of you to God as an instrument for doing right. [14] For sin will not lord over you, for you are not under law but under grace.

This text addresses a problem about how Christians should live. How shall we live, given what God has done in Christ? There is still sin in the world, and there always will be. The presence of evil means evil is always an option. It also means evil is always a threat to life. People will die, and some will die from violence, even while they are in union with Christ. Union with Christ does not obliterate the old age, but it offers a new identity defined by the new age. Union does not mean one is always on a spiritual high. It means that no matter what, you are not alone; no matter what, you can only fall so far; no matter what, God is still for you and with you, goes with you and enables you through all trauma and heartache, gives you a foundation for living, and has reserved your future in his own presence.

Romans 6 shows how Christians must live in this overlap of the old and new ages. Baptism points to union with Christ, and that union demands action from believers that includes a new mindset, a new orientation, and new behavior. It demands a fidelity to a new Lord. Fidelity is a helpful word to describe union with Christ. Continuing to live a life of sin is not an option.

In chapter 3 I underscored what this text reveals: baptism is a primary source for participation thinking. *Baptism is at least one source of Paul's "in Christ" theology.* At baptism, believers are "plunged" into Christ to such a degree that they have put on Christ like a garment, as Galatians 3:26–27 puts it. Baptism incorporates believers into Christ, gives them a share in Christ, and establishes a close union with Christ. Paul apparently drew on early-church tradition with such baptismal thinking. Several of his other letters emphasize this teaching, and all of them are heavily about participation with Christ and its results for living (see Rom. 13:14; 1 Cor. 12:12–13; Eph. 4:22–24; Col. 2:12–13; and 3:9–11). These texts are part of Paul's larger focus on dying and rising with Christ. For me, no better portrayal of this theology exists than cross-shaped baptistries from a few centuries after the New Testament (see the photo on p. 43). People took their baptismal identity standing in the middle of the cross. They got it.

Romans 6 is *the* most compelling text on baptism, dying and rising with Christ, being in Christ, and participation. The result is as confident an assertion of the gospel and new life in Christ as any in Scripture. Death is not lord (v. 9), and neither is sin (v. 14). Jesus Christ is (5:21; 6:23). That *is* good news! To be fair, though, this text is not really about baptism. It is about transformed living because of participation with Christ, and baptism is merely the means of making the point.

The focus on participation in 6:1–11 is very strong. In verses 3 and 4 there are three references to "baptized into": verse 3 speaks of being baptized into Christ Jesus, and verses 3 and 4 speak twice of being baptized into his death. As a result of baptism into Christ, there is an emphasis on being *with* Jesus. Five times believers are caught up with Christ in an action that happened to him:[3] they were *buried with Christ* (v. 4), *united with* him (v. 5),[4] and *crucified with* him (v. 6); they *died with* him (v. 8) and *will live with* him

---

3. Four of these are expressed as compounds with the preposition *syn* ("with"). "Died with" in v. 8 is not.

4. The meaning of *symphytoi* is debated. It is used in the sense of "growing together with" and, more generally, of being "united" or "identified with."

(v. 8). Then, in verse 11, comes the command to view yourself as living to God "in Christ Jesus."

The whole point of this passage is that because believers are *joined* with Christ, what happened to him happens to them. Such union with Christ by necessity demands a change in conduct. You cannot go on sinning.

In non-Christian sources *baptizein* is already and frequently a metaphor for death. The language of being "baptized into" is surprising. In ancient sources one finds references to being "baptized into" water in the sense of drowning or a ship sinking, or to being "baptized" into some other liquid, particularly of being baptized into drunkenness, but not being "baptized into death or into a person." The only occurrences of baptism in relation to a person is of a sword or spear being "baptized"—thrust—into someone.[5] "Baptize into" is not frequent in the New Testament,[6] and the intent of the few non-Pauline passages is uncertain. Still, the force of "into" (*eis*) must not be diminished, as if it merely meant "baptize in." This is what translations do with *baptizein eis* ("baptized into") in Matthew 28:19 and elsewhere.[7] Paul's intent is quite clear. Baptism moves one *into* Christ. It is directional, incorporative, eschatological, and a life-changing event. The baptized are made one with Christ and become part of him, part of his body, united to other believers in him.[8]

The ritual is *not merely a symbol* and is not magic. Rightly understood, baptism marks a profound union with Christ. It *enacts* dying and rising with Christ and expresses the movement into a

---

5. See, e.g., Josephus, *Jewish War* 2.476.

6. See Matt. 28:19; Mark 1:9 (into the Jordan); Acts 8:16; 19:3–5; Rom. 6:3–4; 1 Cor. 1:13, 15; 10:2; 12:13; and Gal. 3:27. "Baptized into Moses" in 1 Cor. 10:2 is an imprecise analogy meant to prevent any idea that baptism is a magical rite, as if to say, "These people had a similar water experience in relation to Moses, but it did not save them."

7. The NRSV and NIV have done the same at Mark 1:9; Acts 8:16; and 19:3–5 but not for 1 Cor. 10:2; 12:13; and Gal. 3:27, except that in 1 Cor. 12:13 the NIV has changed "into one body" (NIV 1984) to "to form one body" (NIV 2011).

8. See esp. 1 Cor. 12:12–13; Gal. 3:26–29; Col. 2:12–13; and 3:9–11.

new sphere for living. The baptized are no longer in sin or under
the law. They live somewhere else. They have been moved into the
sphere of Christ's existence, his death, and his life so that they
live under grace (Rom. 6:14). They live in a new environment. To
express it another way, they have been decentered from themselves
and re-centered in Christ.[9]

Baptism expresses so close an involvement and *solidarity* with
Christ that one owns and participates in the narrative of his death
and his life. What happened to Christ happens to believers. The
language is different from "one died for all; therefore, all died"
(2 Cor. 5:14), but the thought is the same. What else could "baptized into his death" mean except that one was taken into his death
and died with him in order to live with him? The passives "we
were baptized" and "we were buried" are divine passives indicat-
ing that God did the action. We did not place ourselves in Christ.
God's Spirit put us there, but we still have a role. If we do not act,
nothing will happen. Remember that in our response to God, God
is already at work engaging us and enlisting our response. But we
still have to respond.

That is why the statement in Romans 6:11 is so important:
"Consider yourselves dead in relation to sin but alive in Christ
Jesus in relation to God." This new mindset and new orientation
mean the connection to sin and the tyranny of sin are broken. The
new mindset must be implemented. One must actually live from
the conviction that what God has said is true, and such living is
an essential aspect of faith. One cannot go on living as if nothing
has happened to change the relation to sin.

Some questions about baptism may never be solved. Is God's
act in the ritual, or does the ritual mirror the divine act that has
already occurred? We separate baptism and faith, but I doubt the

9. Drawing on Volf's comment, which was quoted above (p. 48): "Paul presumes a
centered self, more precisely a *wrongly* centered self that needs to be de-centered by
being nailed to the cross. . . . The self is never without a center; it is always engaged in
the production of its own center." Miroslav Volf, *Exclusion and Embrace* (Nashville:
Abingdon, 1996), 69 (italics original).

early church did. Regardless of the questions and debates, however, we must never lose focus on the theology of baptism. Baptism points to the reality of being taken into Christ and given a share with him for transformed living. Let the debates diminish in importance, and hold firmly to the theology of dying and rising with Christ.

The noun *pistis* ("faith") does not occur in this section and, in fact, surprisingly, does not occur between Romans 5:1 and 9:30, almost five chapters![10] The verb *pisteuein* ("have faith" or "believe") occurs in 6:8 but nowhere else between 4:24 and 9:33. Chapters 5–8 are focused more on participation language, but they do not suggest a different relation to God than faith language does. Faith in Christ means a person identifies with Christ's death and resurrection and is bound to him, which is the focus in 6:1–14. Faith in Christ *is* participation with Christ, being bound relationally to him. This is Paul's understanding of the meaning of faith, as the use of *symphytoi* in 6:5 shows, regardless of whether one understands the term as "grafted onto" or merely "united with."[11]

In 6:2–8 the emphasis is on death, the *believer's* death (death to sin and in identification with Christ's death); being buried with Christ; being joined to his death; and being crucified with him. In 6:4b and 9–10, the focus is on Christ's defeat of death so that death no longer dominates. All this emphasis on death has one purpose: human transformation that dethrones sin. Dying with Christ means dying to sin and not living as slaves under its control (v. 6). The tyrant sin is no longer lord.

Martin Luther understood this and taught that "a truly Christian life is nothing else than a daily baptism."[12] To live our baptism

---

10. It does occur as a variant in 5:2.

11. Or "assimilated to." See the discussion by C. E. B. Cranfield, *A Critical and Exegetical Commentary on the Epistle to the Romans*, International Critical Commentary (Edinburgh: T&T Clark, 1975), 1:306–8.

12. Martin Luther, *Large Catechism*, in *The Book of Concord: The Confessions of the Evangelical Lutheran Church*, ed. Robert Kolb and Timothy J. Wengert (Minneapolis: Fortress, 2000), part 4, "Infant Baptism," p. 465.

daily, we must learn how to die continually, which is a metaphorical way of saying we no longer find life centered on ourselves and our own concerns and desires. Paul Minear suggests that instead of looking for evidences of rebirth, we ask how many times a person has died. Rebirth without dying is Christian nonsense, and so is new creation without crucifixion.[13] Dying with Christ and to self is what Christian living is about, but this presumes, as well, rising to newness of life drawn from Christ (6:4).

If Christians are so bound to Christ that they have died with him and rise with him to new life, the ethical consequences are obvious. Human participation with Christ in daily life is the unavoidable response. Grace reigns—dominates (Rom. 5:21)—and believers live under grace (6:14–15), which is another obvious expression of Paul's spheres-of-influence thinking. Christians live in the sphere of God, the Giver, and in the environment of what God has accomplished in Christ. Living under grace assumes participation with the God of grace.

Romans 6 underscores that *life in Christ means participation with God*. Verse 4 indicates that, having died with Christ, and in analogy with his resurrection, we are to walk/live in newness of life. Walking with God is as important a theme in the New Testament as it is in the Old Testament. Here, clearly, that walking has a new sphere, the newness and power brought by Christ's resurrection. According to verse 6 the purpose of being crucified with Christ is to destroy sin's tyranny over the body so that we do not serve sin. Verse 11 directs believers to consider themselves dead to sin but alive to God *in Christ Jesus*. Believers have died with Christ, and they are urged to live from that conviction. The blend of the indicative and the imperative reminds people who God says they are and encourages them to live out that identity.

The verses that follow (vv. 12–13) call for a *revolt* against sin and its misuse of the body and for a refusal to place the body at

13. Paul Minear, *To Die and to Live: Christ's Resurrection and Christian Vocation* (New York: Seabury, 1977), 155.

sin's disposal. Rather, believers are to present themselves to God as those brought from death to life and all of their body as instruments serving what is right (cf. 12:1). The image suggests someone having just been raised from the dead and standing by his or her grave, choosing how the new future will be lived.

With different language these theological convictions are repeated in 6:15–23 and in 7:4–6: freedom from death and sin's dominance, service to and productive living with God because of being in Christ, future resurrection, and eternal life. The words of 7:4–6 serve almost as commentary on 6:1–14. "You" died—this time to the law—through the body of Christ *so that you might be joined to the resurrected one* and "bear fruit" (i.e., live productively) to God.

How does salvation work? By participation, both the participation of God in Christ with us and our participation with Christ in baptism and life. Apart from participation and unity with Christ, salvation cannot take place and does not make sense. To what end is salvation? Life, freedom, newness, productive engagement with what is right and with God, and giving oneself to God and the purposes of God. Salvation and ethics are again part of the same piece of cloth. Romans 6 is *the* text on participation with God in Christ, the good news of participation, and what participation means for how one lives.

1 Corinthians 6:12-20

[12] All things are lawful for me, but not all things are profitable. All things are lawful for me, but I will not be dominated by anything. [13] Food is for the stomach, and the stomach is for food, but God will do away with both. The body is not for sexual sin but for the Lord, and the Lord is for the body. [14] God both raised the Lord and will raise us by his power. [15] Do you not know that your bodies are members of Christ? Shall I take the members of Christ and make them members of a prostitute? No way! [16] Do you not know that

the one joined to a prostitute is one body with her? For it says, "The two will become one flesh." [17] The one being joined to the Lord becomes one spirit with him. [18] Run from sexual sin! Every other sin a person commits is outside the body, but the one committing sexual sin sins against his or her own body. [19] Do you not know that your body is a temple of the Holy Spirit in you, the Spirit you have from God, and you do not own yourself? [20] You were bought with a price. Therefore, glorify God in your body.

This text is astonishing because of the extent to which participation with Christ is assumed. As in Ephesians 2:4–10, identification with the death of Christ is not in this passage, and death is not even mentioned. No doubt, the death of Christ is presupposed in 6:11 ("You were acquitted in/by the name of the Lord Jesus Christ") and 6:20 ("You were bought with a price"). Like Romans 6 this passage emphasizes the resurrection, the human *body*, and *what believers do with their bodies*. In other words, the focus is especially on the ethical implications of participation.

The statement in 6:12 "All things are lawful for me" reflects at least a misunderstanding of Christian freedom on the part of the Corinthians. Paul does not correct the statement, but he sets it aside in favor of what is beneficial and to reject that anything might control him, including, specifically, food or sexual sin. The obvious assumption is that only Jesus is Lord. It is clear as the passage unfolds that the real concern here is sexual sin (although food returns as the subject in chaps. 8–10). The surprising thing about verse 13 is that participation is not about some "spiritual" attachment to Christ; it is specifically participation of one's *body*. The body is not for sexual sin or food or anything else rooted merely in our desires, but the body is for the Lord, and the Lord is for the body. The body belongs to the Lord, and the Lord in a real sense belongs to the body, not in the sense that the body owns the Lord but in the sense that the Lord has given himself to bodies so that they are determined by him, very much as in Romans 6.

The statement that the Lord is for the body is a striking statement about God's interest in and care for our physical being. This thinking about our bodies is based in the resurrection of Jesus and the expectation of a resurrection like his for future believers (v. 14).

If this sense of our bodies participating with Christ sounds repressive and limiting of our lives, we have grossly misunderstood both life and Paul. Life is relational, and it is not merely about our relation with ourselves. For Paul, participation with Christ is the only place for freedom, freedom to be who God created us to be, and for healthy, productive living. Paul was not bound, and would not be dominated, by anything—except his relation to Christ.

But the text says more. Your bodies do not merely belong to Christ; they are *part of him* (v. 15). Do not miss this. We have seen this before, and it is emphasized here. Christian faith for Paul means participating with Christ so deeply that you are part of his being and part of the other people in Christ.[14] If you are a Christian, you are part of Christ. The lone individual cannot be conceived of. This is why the "body" metaphor is a foundational feature of Paul's thought. Salvation occurs because one is part of Christ. It is clear, too, that not just one's mind is connected to Christ. Everything, including one's body, is connected to Christ. This expresses an unparalleled sense of the holiness established for the physical body. The theology of Christ's body and the relation of our bodies to it is both physical and surprising. This is not *merely* a metaphor for Paul. It is a theology of deep participation with Christ.

Participation with Christ is so strong that it should preclude wrong kinds of participation—especially with regard to sexual practice. In dependence on Genesis 2:24, verse 16 views sexual intercourse and being joined to a prostitute as forming one body. Sexual relations are *not* merely physical. They are incorporative and create a bond, a new entity, something about which our

14. See also Eph. 5:30; and Rom. 12:5; Eph. 4:25.

society has no idea. Unexpectedly, the same word used in verse 16 of sexual relations—*kollasthai*—is used in verse 17 of being joined to Christ. Participation with Christ, too, is incorporative and creates a new entity made possible by the Spirit.[15] This is a New Testament version of what we saw with the word *dabaq* in Deuteronomy and elsewhere.[16] Faith means being joined to, clinging to, Christ. This being joined to Christ creates a unity with Christ that is described as "one spirit" with Christ (v. 17). How can we do justice to this oneness?

The rest of the text underscores that participation is deeply physical. Our physical body is a temple, a place of dwelling for God's Spirit, with the result that we are not our own. The body is the place to honor and mirror God's own character, very much like the call in Romans 6:13 to present ourselves to God as raised from the dead and our members as instruments for doing right. Once again we see the displacing of the self and the recentering on Christ.

We should notice how much sexual sin is a concern in Scripture, especially in Paul's Letters. Depending on how one counts, the New Testament has about fifteen vice lists—things that do not fit with Christ. Twelve list sexual sin, six of them putting it first. Sometimes two or three different words for sexual sin are given in one list (note, e.g., 1 Cor. 6:9–10 and Gal. 5:19). In our day, sometimes attitudes toward sexual practice in the church are not much different from the rest of the society. In the first century, the arena where Christians were most unlike their neighbors was in sexual practice. Larry Hurtado says, "It is fair to judge that the impact of the distinctive stance of early Christian teaching involved a transformation in the deep logic of sexual morality."[17]

---

15. The Greek translation of Gen. 2:24 uses the compound form *proskollasthai*. In 1 Cor. 6:16 the sexual relation forms "one body." In v. 17 relation with Christ forms "one spirit," but it is precisely a result of a bodily participation with Christ. For a similar "one spirit" idea, see John 3:6.

16. See pp. 66–67.

17. Larry W. Hurtado, *Destroyer of the Gods: Early Christian Distinctiveness in the Roman World* (Waco: Baylor University Press, 2016), 171.

This is the arena where people still are most likely to go "off the rails," but sexual sin is still sin. Christians need to recover this transformation in the deep logic of sexual morality. The depth of participation thinking in 1 Corinthians 6 requires both better thinking and better practice regarding sexual activity. Christians have too often allowed the entertainment media to determine sexual ethics—or destroy sexual ethics—but being joined to Christ redraws and controls all ethical practice, all boundaries, and all relations, especially sexual relations.

The ethical implications of participation with Christ, then, are enormous, and the implied question is this: To what action or commitment will you attempt to join Jesus Christ? Would you really attempt to join Christ to sexual sin? Some things—many things—just do not fit, and the attempt to make them fit brings a ringing "No way!"[18] In fact, the purpose of the virtue and vice lists in the New Testament, texts like Galatians 5:17–23 and Colossians 3:5–17, is to show what does and does not fit in a life joined to Christ. The point is that being in Christ sets ethical boundaries that must not be violated. Christ himself determines the boundaries within which we live. If we are Christians, our every action and thought involves Christ and is determined by him. Union with Christ is not a part-time unity. In a real sense Christ is—or should be—the origin and recipient of every act. To what will you attempt to connect Christ, justifying the action with flawed logic? Will you glorify God with your *body*?

How does salvation work? Only by participation with Christ, the expression of God's love. To what end? Transformation and productive living in relation to God. By necessity, salvation involves ethical transformation.

But can we handle living rigorously all the time? Won't we just get worn out and miss the joy of life? Most of us are nowhere close to finding out. Perhaps "rigorousness" is not the right word, not even for translating Kierkegaard. The Christian life is about joy,

---

18. My translation of Paul's *mē genoito* at the end of v. 15.

not gloom, but Christianity insists that joy is found only in relation to a God who gives himself and not in some kind of self-centered existence. It insists that life requires a seriousness, an alertness, an investment that enhances relation with God, attention to and monitoring of oneself, and attention to other people. How could this not be so when all of life is relational? Christianity also insists that all of life must be heeded, not just the present moment of one's desires. Life is seriously serious, and the failure to recognize that will destroy any thought of joy. Joy is found not in self-focus but in life with God. Jesus's discipleship saying reminds us that the one wishing to save life loses it and the one who loses it for his sake and the gospel's saves it.[19] He came that we may have life abundantly (John 10:10), real life filled with meaning, purpose, and joy.

Still, how can we know enough and be wise enough to deal with all the issues in the New Testament and all the problems in life? We do not need to know everything or deal with everything. As Psalm 103:13–14 reminds us, the Lord knows how we are made and is full of mercy. The way Paul deals with the failures of early Christians like the Corinthians is instructive. No one is expected to be a superhuman. Grace and forgiveness are always in full force, but not where people take them for granted. The important point made repeatedly is that being in Christ sets the parameters for living. There is not a lower standard, nor is there fear or a dread of failure. Rather, the focus is on freedom, joy, and hope, knowing that life is derived from Christ and not from oneself.

What Does This Mean for Individual Christians?[20]

Many other texts in Paul could and should be included, not least 1 Corinthians 10:16–17, with its focus on the Lord's Supper being

---

19. See Matt, 16:25/Mark 8:35/Luke 9:24/John 12:25.
20. Remembering, of course, that there is no such thing as a mere individual and that we are relational beings.

a participation in the death and body of Christ. See also such crucial texts as Galatians 2:16–21; Philippians 3:1–11; and Colossians 2:6–3:11. These and other texts express Paul's convictions about dying and rising with Christ. Some of the texts treated above do not focus on dying with Christ. Galatians 2:16–21 does not mention rising with Christ. Even though Paul emphasizes that Christ lives in him, his primary focus in this text is on having been crucified with Christ. Paul is so convinced of this that he can say he is *no longer living* and that the life he now lives "in the flesh" (i.e., in his body) he lives by faith in (or the faithfulness of) Christ. This "I, not I" stance, as some describe it, raises questions. How much is an obliteration of Paul's own being—and ours—involved in being crucified with Christ? At one level—that of an independent existence based on one's own desires—completely, but at another level Paul is still an agent who can and must act.

An overemphasis on "total depravity" leads to total uselessness. It is much better to think of pervasive depravity than total depravity. Pervasive depravity recognizes that sin infects *all* our being and requires God's help in *all* our being but that it is also this very being that God calls to participate with him. Participation thinking sets aside much of the sovereignty of God–versus–human action debate,[21] for can one participate with God as a result of God's grace and not act in accord with God?

Still, how should we discuss issues about human responsibility and action? First, regarding responsibility, some speak as if humans cannot respond, as if they are merely victims of the powers of sin and death. This "apocalyptic" approach has merit, but it is one-sided. It again suggests lone individuals unable to resist the powers, and that is true *if* one is analyzing human ability cut off from God. But humans cannot legitimately be conceived of as cut off from God. God is always engaged with us and expects us to respond to his presence and call. Certainly, this does not

21. See pp. 71–72 on the Old Testament and pp. 111–14 on Acts.

give anyone a claim on God or create some independent basis for identity or value on one's own, but if humans are completely powerless to act, what is the purpose of all the commands, the instructions for living, and the warnings of judgment? Why is there such a command as "Lay hold on eternal life" (1 Tim. 6:12)? Even in responding to God, we are not on our own, but we do indeed have responsibility and will be held accountable for it.

There is no loss of individuality. For all of his dying with Christ, Paul was still alive. He was Paul, not Peter, and still had his own characteristics and responsibilities, which in Christ were made subservient to Christ. As much as some might be attracted to the idea "It is all Jesus and none of me," that is not true. Karl Barth says, "The formula 'God everything and man nothing' as a description of grace is not merely a 'shocking simplification' but complete nonsense."[22]

It is still the specific "I"—the specific individual, who is unlike every other individual—who must act and, in doing so, expresses a specific identity. Even the "I" who chooses to identify with the death and resurrection of Jesus and undergoes death is still a singular individual animated by Christ's Spirit. What that person does on behalf of Christ is still legitimately honored by others and will be honored by God.

Paul honored any number of people for their service or leadership, viewed Andronicus and Junia as well esteemed among the apostles (Rom. 16:7), and could look back on his own life and say, "I have fought the good fight. I have finished the race. I have kept the faith" (2 Tim. 4:7–8).[23] Such assessments do not become the basis of identity or value, for all is a gift of grace (1 Cor. 4:7), but neither are they considered of no consequence. Such assessments are evidence of a valid participation with Christ where life

22. Karl Barth, *Church Dogmatics* IV/1, *The Doctrine of Reconciliation*, trans. G. W. Bromiley (Edinburgh: T&T Clark, 1956), 89, quoted in Adam Neder, *Participation in Christ: An Entry into Karl Barth's "Church Dogmatics,"* Columbia Series in Reformed Theology (Louisville: Westminster John Knox, 2009), 50.
23. See also the confidence of such texts as 1 John 3:19–24.

is engaged and experienced, not merely observed, but also where individuals make decisions and live out their existence in Christ. This focus on individuals does not suggest individualism, for being in Christ, by necessity, is communal in that people belong to each other because they belong to Christ. But it is as *individuals* that they belong to each other.

Note the assessment of John Barclay: "It appears that human agency is the *necessary expression* of the life of the Spirit, and certainly not its antithesis; the two are not mutually exclusive as if in some zero-sum calculation. Paul's central theology of participation requires that human agency is reconceived without being abandoned, the self not merely relocated but reconstituted by its absorption within the *non-coercive power of grace.*"[24]

Second, serious attention must be given to the *necessity of action.* Attachment to Christ creates action with Christ. There is no such thing as an identity that does not act or a creature without energy and movement. All things do indeed receive the characteristics of that in which they participate,[25] and if you participate with Christ, you must take on the characteristics and concerns of Christ—and act. What else could "Jesus is Lord" mean? There is no thought of perfectionism, for while sin is not lord, it is still present as an option. Sin will occur because of our limited vision, our limited understanding, our blindness, our failures, our pride, and our biases toward ourselves, but it will not be descriptive of our way of life or dominate who we are.

With actions we are not speaking merely of physical acts. Focusing your life is an act; conscious thought and speaking are acts. Study and learning are acts, even acts of worship. But by necessity, all such mental acts have to result in physical actions. In our

---

24. John M. G. Barclay, "'By the Grace of God, I Am What I Am': Grace and Agency in Philo and Paul," in *Divine and Human Agency in Paul and His Cultural Environment,* ed. John M. G. Barclay and Simon Gathercole (London: T&T Clark, 2006), 140–57, here 156 (italics original).

25. Robert Letham, *Union with Christ in Scripture, History, and Theology* (Phillipsburg, NJ: P&R, 2011), 93.

overburdened fear of salvation by works and works righteousness, we have denigrated the necessity of action. If you do not act in keeping with Christ, you cannot be—and are not—part of Christ.

This is not a new idea, but why actions have been so denigrated is a mystery. Why do we so easily tear apart being, thinking, and doing? No serious Christian thinker can be satisfied with the separation. Kierkegaard says, "God is worshiped not by moods but by action," "Christianity in motion is Christianity," and, "As for the life of the rigorously religious person, his life is essentially action."[26] This should be true of all who really believe. Barclay is in firm agreement with Kierkegaard: "It is *in practice*, both individual and communal, that the reality of the Christ-event is either articulated or denied."[27] Many others have said the same kind of thing. If Christians do not demonstrate the gospel by their lives, they have not understood their own gospel.

To revisit the question "To what end?" the purpose of salvation is not so you can go to heaven. It is that you may live with Christ. Going to heaven is just not the biblical focus. Resurrection and life with God in the future are indeed the expectation, but most of the attention in the New Testament is on transformation of life in the present, and that can be shown only by action. The purpose of the saving work of God is to defeat sin and establish right living.

Of the four texts we have examined more closely, only 1 Corinthians 6:12–20 mentions the Holy Spirit, but the Spirit is always at the center of Paul's thinking, as is evident in the larger context

---

26. Søren Kierkegaard, *Søren Kierkegaard's Journals and Papers*, ed. Howard V. Hong and Edna H. Hong (Bloomington, IN: Indiana University Press, 1967), 1:9, 155; and Kierkegaard, *For Self-Examination; Judge for Yourself!*, ed. and trans. Howard V. Hong and Edna H. Hong, Kierkegaard's Writings 21 (Princeton: Princeton University Press, 1990), 11.

27. John M. G. Barclay, *Paul and the Gift* (Grand Rapids: Eerdmans, 2015), 429 (italics original). See also Barclay, "Under Grace: The Christ-Gift and the Construction of a Christian *Habitus*," in *Apocalyptic Paul: Cosmos and Anthropos in Romans 5–8*, ed. Beverly Roberts Gaventa (Waco: Baylor University Press, 2013), 59–76; see esp. 73–76.

of each of these texts. One does not start with Jesus and then get the Spirit. *All* of Christian existence directly involves the Spirit. Conversion happens only because the Spirit has poured out the love of God in our hearts (Rom. 5:5). It is the law of the Spirit of life in Christ Jesus that has freed us from the law of sin and death (Rom. 8:2). We are wrong if we think that conversion happens one way and then something else takes over for living. Paul asks in Galatians 3:3, "Having begun by the Spirit, will you now be completed by the flesh?" His point is that the means of beginning the faith—that is, the Spirit—is also the means for living the faith. All the discussion above about individual responsibility and the necessity of action are grounded in Paul's heavy emphasis on the Spirit as the motivation, energy, and participant of all Christian living. To put it another way, the means of Christ's ongoing participation with us is the Spirit, for the Spirit is the presence of Christ in his absence.[28]

---

28. This is Raymond E. Brown's definition of the word *paraklētos*, John's term for the Spirit in John 14–16. See Brown, *The Gospel according to John*, Anchor Bible (Garden City, NY: Doubleday, 1966), 2:1141.

ten

Striking Assertions
of Participation

Indeed, the mystery of Christ runs the risk of being disbelieved
precisely because it is so incredibly wonderful.

Cyril of Alexandria[1]

As if texts like 1 Corinthians 6:12–20 were not astonishing
enough, still other texts are so bold in describing participation
that they almost take one's breath. Are they just exaggerations?
Can they be grasped? Some of these texts are slighted because
they appear in "lesser parts" of the canon. Some may not be taken
seriously because the language is so familiar that few reflect on
their intent. Three groups of texts have what I consider striking
assertions: texts on ingesting God or Christ, texts in Hebrews
on Christ's participation with us by taking on flesh, and texts
from 1 and 2 Peter, the latter describing Christians as *partakers*
of the divine nature.

1. Saint Cyril of Alexandria, *On the Unity of Christ*, trans. John McGuckin
(Crestwood, NY: St. Vladimir's Seminary Press, 1995), 61.

Ingesting God or Christ

These are texts that may be so familiar that we take them for granted, but they are astonishing. They are "only metaphors"; should they be taken seriously? They must be taken seriously, for they express fundamental ideas of relation to God.

Prophetic texts sometimes express receiving revelation from God in terms of eating a word or scroll from God to emphasize the impact of and internalization of the message. Jeremiah 15:16, for example, says, "Your words were found, and I ate them."[2] That is odd enough, but we would not expect the idea of ingesting—eating or drinking—God or Christ. Both Testaments use this imagery. It is a huge indicator of the depth and seriousness with which the writers understood participation. They knew believing meant taking God or Christ into one's very being and finding in their Lord the sustenance and direction needed for life and identity.

Several texts, especially in the Psalms, use ingesting imagery to express desire for God, dependence on God, and blessing from God. As examples, note the following (all from the NRSV):

Psalm 34:8: "Taste and see that the LORD is good." (First Peter 2:3 adapts these words and applies them to Christ. Christians, nourished by "spiritual milk" (v. 2), are described as those who have tasted that the Lord is good. This is not an allusion to the Eucharist. It is a way to express the extent to which Christ is taken into and nourishes one's being.)

Psalm 36:8–9: "They feast on the abundance of your house, and you give them drink from the river of your delights. For with you is the fountain of life; in your light we see light."

Psalm 42:1–2: "As a deer longs for flowing streams, so my soul longs for you, O God. My soul thirsts for God, for the living God."

2. See also Isa. 55:1–11; Jer. 1:9; Ezek. 2:8–3:3; Ps. 119:103; and Prov. 9:5 (of wisdom).

Psalm 63:1: "O God, you are my God, I seek you, my soul thirsts for you; my flesh faints for you, as in a dry and weary land where there is no water."[3]

Jeremiah 2:13: "My people have committed two evils: they have forsaken me, the fountain of living water, and dug out cisterns for themselves, cracked cisterns that can hold no water."[4]

In the New Testament the imagery of ingesting Jesus is more explicit and is most obvious in John. In 4:10–15 Jesus is the source of living water. Worth noting is 4:32–34, where Jesus says he has food from the Father, which includes doing the will of the Father. This is not ingesting, but it is still important, for his desire to obey God nourishes his being.

Most blatant on ingesting Jesus is John 6:27–63, which views Jesus first as bread of life given from heaven and asserts that the one coming and believing in him will never hunger or thirst (v. 35). Those eating this bread gain eternal life. Toward the end of the passage, the emphasis is on eating his flesh and drinking his blood. His flesh is true food, and his blood is true drink. The one eating his flesh and drinking his blood *remains* in Jesus and Jesus in that person (vv. 55–56). The text is about participation.

This is not a eucharistic text, even if it is secondarily applicable to the Eucharist. It is a text about ingesting Jesus and finding life. Those who ingest Jesus take him into their being and are bound to him relationally, and the living Christ communicates life to them. The language is a substitute for language of believing. Belief binds people so closely to Jesus it is as if they have ingested him. John 7:37–39 repeats these ideas by saying those thirsting are to come and drink from Jesus, for rivers of living water flow from him.[5]

3. See also Pss. 68:26 and 143:6.
4. See also Jer. 17:13 and Isa. 55:1–2.
5. Some translations punctuate the text differently so that the living waters flow from the believer, but this is a mistake. See also Rev. 22:17.

Paul is just as much at home with ingesting imagery. In 1 Corinthians 10:2–4, in saying Israelites at the exodus experienced something parallel to baptism and Eucharist, he says that the Israelites had spiritual drink from the rock that followed them and that this rock was Christ.[6] More importantly, later in the chapter (vv. 16–17) he views observance of the Lord's Supper as a *koinōnia*—a joint sharing or participation—with the blood and body of Christ.

Whatever else is said, early Christians viewed themselves as bound so closely to their Lord that he invaded their being and provided the sustenance from which they lived. Their lives drew from and shared his life. They lived participation.

Hebrews: Christ's Participation by Taking on Flesh

Hebrews has neither "in Christ" nor dying and rising with Christ, and it does not even mention the resurrection of Jesus, although obviously this is assumed with the heavy focus on his being seated at the right hand of God, as in 1:3 and elsewhere. Hebrews, however, has a heavy focus on Jesus's participation with humanity, his atoning death for them, and his high priesthood for them. By God's grace he tasted death for all (2:9), which sounds very close to "One died for all; therefore, all died" (2 Cor. 5:14).

The astonishing part for me is the focus on Christ's participation with humanity via the incarnation. He called humans "brothers and sisters" (2:11), shared (*meteschen*) flesh and blood with them to defeat the power of death (2:14), became like them in every respect to atone for their sins (2:17), and suffered and was tempted that he might help those who are tempted (2:18). This emphasis on Christ's ability to sympathize with the weakness of humans is also in 4:15, which says he was tempted in every respect like them but was without sin. He came alongside us because of God's love

---

6. With "the rock that followed," Paul adapts a widely attested Jewish tradition. See the treatment by David E. Garland, *1 Corinthians*, Baker Exegetical Commentary on the New Testament (Grand Rapids: Baker Academic, 2003), 455–58.

for humanity. The emphasis on Christ as the high priest, identifying with his people and offering himself for them, also strongly expresses participation (see esp. 9:24–28). This is not some remote connection; it is a caring, sympathetic engagement with and on behalf of people. It demonstrates again how much God is for us.

Hebrews also views Christ as dwelling in his people. Hebrews 3:6 contrasts Moses, a servant in God's house, with Christ, who is a son in God's house, and then asserts that *we are his house* if we hold firmly to the boldness and confidence (literally "boasting") based on hope. Those who live faithfully are a house in which Christ lives, an image that is reminiscent of language describing Christians as a temple in which God dwells (Eph. 2:19–22 and 1 Pet. 2:4–5). A bit later, in 3:14, as he encourages people to persevere, the writer provides a strong and explicit text on participation: "We have become sharers of / participants with [*metochoi*] Christ if we hold our original commitment firmly to the end." This text does not receive its due. It is a bold assertion of having a share in Christ, participating with Christ, which is similar to sharing in the Spirit in 6:4. The writer seems to take participation for granted.

Participation in 1 and 2 Peter

1 Peter. The most astonishing part of the participation thinking in 1 and 2 Peter is the idea of partaking of the divine nature found in 2 Peter 1:3–4, but it is surprisingly strong in 1 Peter as well. The emphasis on identification with God in 1:15–16 attracts attention: "As the one who called you is holy, you be holy . . . just as has been written, 'You will be holy because I am holy.'"[7] The thought here is what we have seen before and is the assumption of all Scripture: God's people will take their character from their God.

Above we mentioned the ingesting language in 1 Peter 2:3, and the participation ideas continue in 2:4–5, where Christ is described

---

7. The quotation is from Lev. 19:2.

as a living stone to whom believers come—continually. The "stone" imagery is drawn from several Old Testament texts, which are quoted in verses 6–8, and "living" is a pointer to Jesus's resurrection. Christians are then described as living stones because of their association with him. They live because he lives, and they draw life from him. Because of their connection to him and identity of being like him, they are built into a spiritual house for a holy priesthood that offers spiritual sacrifices pleasing to God. That it is a spiritual house is a result of the activity of the Holy Spirit (cf. Eph. 2:19–22). That both Christ and believers are called living stones is only one example of something being said of Jesus that is then also said of believers.[8] One can almost hear the later assertion, "He became what we are in order that we might become what he is."[9]

In 1 Peter 2:21–25 participation appears again. Christians, specifically slaves, are called to identify with the suffering of Jesus and follow in his footsteps. Were this the only statement, we might think this views Jesus merely as an example, but verse 24 shows more is involved. This verse is about Christ's identification with us, bearing our sins on the cross—"by his wounds you were healed." But it is also about our identification with Christ by dying to sin and living for righteousness. While this mirrors Paul's dying and rising theology, it uses a different word for dying (*apoginesthai* instead of one of Paul's death terms like *apothnēskein*). Obviously, the theology is not limited to slaves.

A few other participation texts occur in the rest of the letter. There are three occurrences of "in Christ": 3:16, "your good conduct in Christ"; 5:10, "God . . . who called you to his eternal glory in Christ"; and 5:14, "Peace to all those in Christ." As with Paul and John, "in Christ" occurs without explanation, as language that people took for granted. Participation with Christ's sufferings

---

8. Other examples of something being said of both Jesus and the believers include the following: He is the anointed one, and Christians are called anointed (2 Cor. 1:21 and 1 John 2:20, 27). He is called "God's beloved," and so are Christians (Rom. 1:7 and Eph. 5:1). He laid down his life for others, and Christians are to do the same (1 John 3:16).

9. On this quotation, see p. 27 and p. 46, n. 20.

appears again at 4:13, this time with the verb *koinōnein* ("share," "participate"). Rejoicing in participation with his sufferings now will, when he is revealed in glory, result in overwhelming joy. Then, in 5:12, the author affirms that the letter is the true grace of God, in which the readers stand/live. This expresses the same spheres of existence that dominate so much of Paul's thinking. The closest parallel is Romans 5:2.[10]

2 Peter 1:3–4. Second Peter may be short and often ignored, but *it has the most explicit description of participation in Scripture.* At least that is what the Orthodox Church believes. The words bear quotation:

> As his divine power has given us all things pertaining to / needed for godly living through the knowledge of the one who called us by his own glory and excellence, through these things he has given us his great and valuable promises, that through these things you become *sharers of the divine nature*, since you have escaped from the corruption in the world based in lust. (1:3–4)

Sharing in the divine nature may shock some, but clearly this author took participation with God very seriously. We saw this thinking expressed with different words in John 17, and such expressions led the church fathers to emphasize sharing *in God*.[11] From our treatment so far, this assertion should not be a surprise, nor should these verses be seen as odd or inferior. They are often associated with the emphasis in the Orthodox Church on *theosis*, or deification, but whether such terms are helpful and just what is meant by them are debated.[12]

Do Christians really share in God's nature? If we take conversion seriously, we must say "Yes!" Other texts may not use this

---

10. See pp. 18–19.
11. See pp. 27–29.
12. For an overview, see the articles in Michael J. Christensen and Jeffrey A. Wittung, eds., *Partakers of the Divine Nature: The History and Development of Deification in the Christian Traditions* (Grand Rapids: Baker Academic, 2008).

language, but they point to the same reality. Think again of texts like Ezekiel 36:25–27 (which promises the Spirit will give a new heart and a new spirit), John 3:6 ("That which is born from the merely human [the flesh] is merely human. That which is born from the Spirit is spirit"), and Romans 8:6 (which contrasts living according to that which is merely human [the flesh] with living by the Spirit). By necessity, being joined to God in faith brings the impact of God's character.

But what does it mean to partake of God's nature? Key in the discussion is the timing of when such participation with God takes place. Some think the language of sharing in the divine nature is merely a way to talk about escaping mortality (becoming immortal) at the resurrection in the future and does not relate to present deification.[13] The difference of opinion is evident in the NRSV and NIV translations of 2 Pet. 1:4.

> NRSV: ". . . his precious and very great promises, so that through them you *may* escape from the corruption that is in the world because of lust, and may become participants of the divine nature."

> NIV: ". . . his very great and precious promises, so that through them you may participate in the divine nature, *having escaped* the corruption in the world caused by evil desires."

In the latter, as in my translation above, the escape has already taken place, and one already shares in the divine nature. Good reasons exist for seeing this as the intent. The aorist participle for "escaped" (*apophygontes*) would more likely point to a past event, and in 2:20 the same participle reappears and refers to having escaped shameful deeds in the present life. Given the parallels between the two sections, most likely the emphasis in 1:4 is on the

---

13. See Richard J. Bauckham, *Jude, 2 Peter*, Word Biblical Commentary 50 (Waco: Word, 1983), 180–82. Bauckham thinks 2 Pet. 1:3–4 (and a lot more) reflects Hellenistic thinking about escaping mortality. For him the verses are not about participation in God but about sharing in the nature of heavenly, immortal beings. To share God's nature is to become immortal.

present moral life. This is confirmed by the focus on the present life that precedes and follows verse 4, on everything given to us for godly living in verse 3, and on a series of cascading ethical expectations in verses 5–8, ending in verse 8 where it began in verse 3, with the knowledge of Jesus Christ. Obviously, 2 Peter has a focus on future eschatology, but not in these verses, except indirectly.[14] Also, since it is widely acknowledged that 2 Peter reflects Hellenistic language, we should note that in the Greco-Roman world, typically language about sharing in the divine nature is about this present life.[15] Sharing in the divine nature in 2 Peter is a privilege available during life, and no doubt, believers will share in God's immortal nature in the new heavens and new earth (3:13), but this is not explicitly stated.

But still, what does it mean to share in the divine nature? Such language could easily be misunderstood as arrogant or cultlike, but it is nothing of the sort. It has nothing to do with the divine essence of God, any thought of surpassing the characteristics that distinguish God and humanity, any idea of a semidivine amalgamation, or the idea that humans attain some superhuman nature. Sharing the divine nature has its roots in humanity in the image of God (Gen. 1:26–27), and as the context overwhelmingly shows, the focus is on mirroring the *moral* characteristics of God. Again, as everywhere in Scripture, God's people are to take their character from their God, and the Christian ethic is always a reflective, responsive ethic. It reflects the character of God and is a response to God's initial action, which is strongly emphasized in 2 Peter 1:3–4. Participation with God and Christ is a moral enterprise. "One is given the ability to live virtuously."[16] This ability is a gift resulting

14. The promises in v. 3 could be with regard to the end time or to the present.
15. See Plato, *Theaetetus* 176ab; Seneca, "On the Happy Life," *Epistle* 92.30; Appian, *Hannabalic War* 2; Philo, *Allegorical Interpretation* 1.38; Josephus, *Against Apion* 1.232; and Ignatius, *To the Ephesians* 4.2. Fourth Maccabees 18:3 is about the future.
16. James M. Starr, *Sharers in Divine Nature: 2 Peter 1:4 in Its Hellenistic Context*, Coniectanea Biblica New Testament Series 33 (Stockholm: Almqvist & Wiksell International, 2000), 228.

from God's work in Christ, and because faith joins people to God, they partake of his character.

I do not find *theosis* or deification language particularly helpful, and both can be misleading. On the other hand, properly understood and in keeping with much of the church's tradition, the ideas behind such language are essential. They embody the frequent saying "He became what we are that we might become what he is," as we saw above. Why have a God if that God does not set the direction for your life—and enable it?

eleven

So What?

For Jesus Christ, and our union with him, is the good news. . . .
We would rather have the occasional brush of God's presence, or
a relic of his solidarity with us, so that God can be an appendage
of our identity. But God wants more than that; he wants our lives,
our adopted identity.

J. Todd Billings[1]

The gospel, the gospel we need, is a gospel of participation. The theology of the New Testament is a theology of participation. So what? What difference does a gospel of participation make? Absolutely everything! Not least in getting rid of a gospel that is a farce and makes no difference. You do need a better gospel, the gospel of participation in and with Christ. This is the real gospel and the only legitimate one. Perhaps, with the church now in decline, people will be forced to rethink what they are doing, and the gospel can actually be recovered and taken seriously. Imagine the impact if people actually lived the real gospel.

1. J. Todd Billings, *Union with Christ: Reframing Theology and Ministry for the Church* (Grand Rapids: Baker Academic, 2011), 10, 18 (emphasis original).

When I was a relatively young scholar, I attended the consultation on Matthew at a huge annual meeting of religion and Bible
scholars, a meeting to which about 10,000 scholars come. The
room for the Matthew consultation was packed, with most of us
sitting on the floor and twenty or so primary participants seated
at a large table. There was one empty seat, and the cochair, who
happened to be a friend of mine, motioned that I should move up
to the table. Soon I found myself saying the theory just presented
by a major scholar at the table would not work, something I would
never have done watching from the floor. That led to an invitation
to give a paper the next year. A change in "geography" changed
everything. The point is that participation, being in Christ, engages and enables, whereas watching and thinking about do not
do either and are not effective for much at all. With Christianity,
no one is allowed to sit on the floor and watch. Everyone is invited to the table, and being there gives responsibility. Conversion is such a change in "geography,"[2] so one is moved into the
sphere where Jesus Christ and participation in his life determine
everything.

From our investigation it is evident that Scripture everywhere
emphasizes this participation and that the great thinkers in the
church's history both assume it and seek to explain it. It is evident
as well that participation with Christ is the basis of our salvation
and the power and direction for living.

It does no good merely to affirm all the right doctrines. Knowledge by itself does nothing worthwhile. It must be lived, implemented, experienced, and put into force. This is not to suggest
"life over doctrine." It is to insist on *correct* doctrine, for life flows
from proper understanding. Any doctrine that does not translate
into right living is a heretical doctrine. True orthodoxy is never
about merely thinking right thoughts. It is about thinking rightly
to live rightly.

---

2. Granted, conversion takes place in various ways, but the end result is still living
in Christ and being determined by him.

Everyone admires Jesus, but admiring Jesus is not enough. Remember Søren Kierkegaard's compelling contrast between being an admirer of Christ and being a follower.[3] The admirer can admire from a distance, as if in a theater and safe from any impact, and as if admiring were itself meritorious. The follower, however, seeks to be what he or she admires. For Kierkegaard, Jesus's life was calculated to require followers and to make admirers impossible, and consequently, only the follower is the true Christian. Kierkegaard did not use the language, but he was arguing for a gospel of participation.

So what? God does not desire just that you believe in him. God's desire is that you *live*—walk—with God. The purpose of Scripture is not merely to give you information about God; it is to enable you to live with God. The teaching of the whole of Scripture is this: You were created for participation with God, to live and walk with God, drawing life from his presence. Your life was never intended to be an independent journey on your own. The more it is, the more depressing and meaningless it is. The participation to which we are called is all from grace, all-encompassing, all-motivating, all-engaging, and *completely life-enhancing*. It gives substance, direction, joy, and meaning to life. Participation with God conveys a *dignity* to humans that is unparalleled and breathtaking, but such connection with God is the reason we were created. Participation also has a future component. We will share with the triune God in another way, in his eternal life and glory in his kingdom. We will be like him, for we will see him as he is (1 John 3:2–3; see also Phil. 1:21–23). There is indeed hope.

The Bible has a huge focus on the presence of God in our lives and everywhere assumes that God is with us. That presence requires participation, and *proximity produces impact*. This is true generally; a fire miles away is not like one next door. It is especially true with awareness of the presence of God. If we have some sense

3. See p. 33.

that God is with us, everything changes. Such awareness prevents sin, gives comfort, and motivates love. This is part of the reason for Christianity's focus on the Spirit. The Spirit is the presence of Jesus in his absence, and that presence reorients life.

We are never alone, no matter how wretched life may become. God, the one who chose—and chooses—to draw near to us, who is for us, and who gives and stabilizes life, is with us. You were created for this kind of relation. This is neither some super spirituality nor some emotional experience—although it will include emotion, the amount depending on the person. This is a clear-eyed understanding that life was never intended to take place apart from walking with God, mirroring God, relating to God, and being involved with God and God's purposes. It is a call for trust without presumption—well aware of our need for humility, of our tendency to be self-centered, and that we still live in the old age, even if we are not defined by it.

So what? With participation, the death of Jesus for us and salvation make sense. As we have seen, participation is a huge benefit in thinking theologically about a variety of subjects: incarnation, salvation, ethics, and the relation of God's action and human action. How does this gospel of participation work? What "mechanism" transfers people from a life of self-centered sin to life with God? God both designed and embodies the mechanism, for God is a reconciling God. God in Christ binds himself to us and seeks that we, through the aid of the Spirit, bind ourselves to him. Salvation neither makes sense nor happens apart from such unity and involvement, and the involvement extends to all we are, think, and do.

Faith includes trust in this message but is also itself, as Martin Luther said, a *taking hold* of Christ.[4] Faith *is* participation, attachment, and loyalty. It is a taking hold of the fact that we are given access to a new geography, to having our lives housed in the life

4. See p. 29.

of Christ. Life is never merely an isolated, individual existence; it is always housed somewhere. Why not live it where it was supposed to be housed, in relation to the God revealed in Jesus Christ? There new creation, transformation, productive living, meaning, and hope all take place.

So what? Participation thinking provides a foundation for understanding life and Scripture. Participation permeates Scripture, but the biblical writers did not set out to write about participation. It was just the assumption of their message. The Old Testament writers confronted problems in Israel, set the parameters for what life with God should be, and expressed their attachment to God and their commitment to his covenant. Participation in life with the God who lived in their midst was the guiding standard. The New Testament writers told the story of Jesus and addressed issues in early Christian churches. Participation with Christ was the purpose of the story and the means and natural thought process for dealing with issues and problems. The only way to address problems was with the gospel. In effect they said, "You have a problem? Deal with it from the gospel of participation." The biblical writers, especially the New Testament writers, breathed participation.

You will participate in something. Will your choice be worthwhile? The New Testament writers knew you would participate in something and usually drew stark contrasts: people live in sin or in righteousness and in Christ (Rom. 6); they live in darkness or in the light (John 3:19), in death or in life (John 5:24). Salvation and conversion are about being rescued—snatched—from the realm of darkness and death and made *participants* in the realm of light and God's kingdom (Col. 1:13).

What will it take for the church to recover this message of participation? What will take the church past its own unthinking superficiality so that Christians care about something other than entertainment and pleasure and actually live productively as followers of Christ? If the gospel of participation is the gospel we need, what will participation with Christ look like and require? If this message is true, so what?

Faith understood as participation will mean that *you view yourself differently*, more seriously, as more worthy of dignity, and as having more purpose—because you are part of Christ. Life is not about you; life is supposed to be about you attached to Jesus Christ. There is no higher honor and basis for life. What will that require?

The first requirement is this: *Invest time in and attention to participation.* We will need to pay attention, real attention, to the Scriptures, to the gospel, and to the meaning of faith. *Read Scripture with a participation lens*, looking for and being sensitive to this focus. Participation requires time with Christ, attention to his teachings and character, and involvement with his concerns. Without investment of time with Christ, we will never participate with him. We will be participating in something else. Faith in Christ presumes investment of time with Christ. How could one possibly think of being in Christ in a way that did not include time with Christ? Thinking, prayer, and Bible reading are the lifeline of participation—with the proviso that being biblical is sometimes not easy, but then much of life is not.

Serious thinking is essential to Christian living. Not everyone will be or should be a scholar, but all Christians need to be much more reflective about the meaning and significance of faith. The failure of many Christians to think seriously and honestly is an embarrassment. We need to evaluate our society and our own lives and the degree to which they fit with or do not fit with the character of Christ.

That may be easy to say, but it involves something deeply personal and addresses each of us individually. If God intends to have a people, do *you* really want to be part of God's people? Saying yes requires honesty, courage, paying attention to ourselves, making investment in learning, and living as God intended. Paying attention to ourselves will mean taking *responsibility* for our own lives. Why do so many distance themselves from themselves, seek to hide from themselves, focusing more on watching other peoples' lives so much that they bypass focus on their own being? Paying attention to other people, even famous ones, does little or nothing to shape us in good ways. Pay attention to *yourself*. As Kierkegaard emphasizes repeatedly, it is as an individual and alone that you will stand before God at judgment.[5]

Consciously or unconsciously, on waking each day we check our environment. What is the weather? Did anything happen during the night that requires attention? We need equally each day to check our Christian environment, reminding ourselves that our lives are in Christ, remembering our identity, and ordering our actions so that we live appropriately.

A life commitment is required, not an emotional decision that has little impact on life. James Moffatt almost a century ago described conventional Christian experience in his time as "an initial spasm followed by chronic inertia."[6] That "conventional" approach has failed, and nobody even listens to it now. A decision that does not transform, even when accompanied by emotion, does not guarantee eternal life. Such an approach fits with nothing in Scripture.

The second requirement is this: *Get your ego out of it*, which is what dying with Christ and to sin is about. If faith is participation with God and Christ through the Spirit, then life is not just about you. Focusing on your own ego will destroy participation, just as it destroys good human relations. "Dying with Christ" and similar expressions reorient us away from ourselves and our

5. This theme recurs throughout Kierkegaard's writings, and he even dedicates his *Upbuilding Discourses* to "that single individual." One of the more compelling passages is found in Søren Kierkegaard, *Upbuilding Discourses in Various Spirits*, ed. and trans. Howard V. Hong and Edna H. Hong, Kierkegaard's Writings 15 (Princeton: Princeton University Press, 1993), 127–54. This "occasional discourse" was often published separately as *Purity of Heart Is to Will One Thing*.

6. James Moffatt, *The General Epistles: James, Peter, and Judas*, Moffatt New Testament Commentary 15 (New York: Harper and Brothers, 1928), 181.

sin to become our true selves, the selves God intended for people who walk with him.

The focus on the ego points to a rearrangement in the mind and a new mindset, the reasons Scripture has so much focus on the mind and its renewal. Participation is not merely mental, but we will go nowhere without the continual renewing of the mind. Numerous texts show this with such expressions as "having judged this," "consider yourself," and so on. Everything flows from the mental, but participation is no more merely mental than the rest of life. Being in Christ may not be literal in any physical sense, but as we saw earlier, it still involves our bodies.[7] Life is about relations and actions resulting from how the mind interprets reality, and the gospel of participation with Christ offers a better and more enjoyable vision of reality.

The third requirement is this: *commit to action*. Do not think you can participate without acting, obeying, investing, doing, and living in keeping with Jesus's life, death, and resurrection. The faith-works dichotomy is one of the biggest distortions in Christian history. You will work, but from what identity and for what purpose? Participation by necessity engages. It must be lived, and the primary means of doing so is mirroring the love of God. It is impossible to live bound to God without being shaped by God. Do not allow passivity, itself a sin, to dominate your life. What will you do to demonstrate that your life is a participation with Christ?

The fourth requirement is this: *change your language*. The force of Scripture is that faith must be understood in terms of solidarity with and participation with Christ. "Participation" and related words are the language the church needs in order to move past the sterility and passivity of common views of faith. This will mean that *evangelism needs to change*. As I indicated before, stop telling people to ask Jesus into their hearts! It is marginally biblical, and it is not working!

7. See pp. 141–43.

What language should we use to convey this better gospel, the gospel of participation? A number of terms have been used throughout this book: "solidarity," "attachment," "unity with," "sharing in," "being in," "incorporation," and "identification," all of which are helpful. John Calvin especially liked the image of engrafting.[8] Some people favor the language of *theosis*, *Christosis*, or deification, but while these terms have value and a legitimate intent, they are not going to help in everyday discourse in a secular world.

I challenge readers, following Luther's example, to find metaphors that convey participation. In the end, however, the word "participation" itself and biblical language used to convey it seem the most useful. The gospel invites people by God's grace to place their lives in Christ's life, to see their lives as housed in him and directed by him, and to live in keeping with his character. When a person commits to life as a daily *walk with God in Christ*, then that person understands the gospel's invitation. When a person realizes that faith means being *housed in Christ*, so that one lives *in Christ* and remains there, as if in a new environment, then that person has grasped the New Testament message. When a person realizes that all of life is lived *with Christ* and is patterned after his death and resurrection, then that person understands both the grace and the demand the gospel brings. Valid evangelism explains both the gift and the challenge of the gospel and invites people to enter into such solidarity, such participation, with the God revealed in Jesus Christ. God wants such participation. There life finds its meaning, purpose, enjoyment, and hope.

Once again, a warning is in order against arrogance, any sense of super spirituality or superior knowledge, or anything that could be considered a position of special privilege. Participation has nothing to do with such arrogance and distorted thinking about oneself—often symbolized in the "health and wealth gospel."

8. See p. 30.

Being joined to Christ does not mean one is exempt from the suffering and difficulty of life. It means that God is present and participates with you in your trauma and gives peace even in the midst of pain.

Too often, even in our supposedly Christian existence, we and our leaders end up self-centered, self-aggrandizing, and self-promoting. Why? Do not forget how pervasive depravity is. The more one focuses on one's own power and privilege, the less one understands participation with Christ.

Do not get any ideas of perfectionism or any notion that you are more spiritual than others. If you understand participation, you will not think such thoughts. Whatever is not an exercise of humility is not Christian, but do understand that Christianity requires a *confident* humility, which is hard for many to comprehend. Christians have every right to be confident but should never be arrogant or self-serving.

Participation with God in Christ is a huge privilege, really good news, something at the very heart of being created in God's image. Do not sacrifice such a privileged participation for something that is no gospel at all. Live participation!

APPENDIX

The Relation of the Gospels of Jesus and Paul

What do the gospels of Jesus and Paul have in common? Some attempt to argue Paul was the inventor of Christianity, which is naive in the extreme, doing justice neither to the early church on which Paul partly relies nor to the features common to the teaching of Jesus and the teaching of Paul. There are differences, such as the way Christology is expressed, but most of the differences stem from different stances chronologically with reference to Jesus's death and resurrection. Note the following common emphases from both Jesus and Paul.

1. The presence of the future, the presence of the kingdom / the new age, right in the midst of the old age.
2. A focus on the Holy Spirit as proof of the presence of the new age.
3. A new covenant established by Jesus Christ, his death, his resurrection, and the pouring out of the Spirit. Forgiveness and redemption are based in Jesus's death.

4. Emphasis on the gospel as the fulfillment of God's promises.

5. A focus on a confrontation with and a conflict with evil.

6. The overwhelming and undeserved love of God, which sometimes Paul expresses with grace language because of the Greco-Roman patronage culture. Jesus does not use grace language to describe the gospel, but he embodies what grace stands for in eating with sinners and other similar actions.

7. An emphasis on the love commands.

8. The assumption that God's people take their character from God and are to live a reflective, responsive ethic.

9. An emphasis on transformation and new life.

10. An ethical standard of righteousness and justice based on Old Testament teachings and the law. This includes the same teaching on sexual sin and divorce.

11. The necessity of obedience.

12. The blend of the indicative and imperative (statement of fact and command). This is more pronounced with Paul and the early church than with Jesus, but it is there in Jesus's teaching (Matt. 5:14–16; 18:23–34).

13. A focus on finding life by losing it, expressed by Paul as dying and rising with Christ.

14. Solidarity with Christ—in the Synoptics, "following"; in John, "remaining in" and with the imagery of the vine and branches; and in Paul's Letters, "in Christ."

15. Concern for both Israel and the world.

16. Concern for the poor.

17. The rejection of racism.

18. An eschatological expectation of the return of Christ to judge and save.

SELECT BIBLIOGRAPHY

Anderson, Cynthia Peters. *Reclaiming Participation: Christ as God's Life for All*. Minneapolis: Fortress, 2014.

Bates, Matthew W. *Salvation by Allegiance Alone: Rethinking Faith, Works, and the Gospel of Jesus the King*. Grand Rapids: Baker Academic, 2017.

Billings, J. Todd. *Calvin, Participation, and the Gift: The Activity of Believers in Union with Christ*. Oxford: Oxford University Press, 2007.

———. *Union with Christ: Reframing Theology and Ministry for the Church*. Grand Rapids: Baker Academic, 2011.

Blackwell, Ben. *Christosis: Pauline Soteriology in Light of Deification in Irenaeus and Cyril of Alexandria*. Wissenschaftliche Untersuchungen zum Neuen Testament 2/314. Tübingen: Mohr Siebeck, 2011.

Braaten, Carl E., and Robert W. Jenson, eds. *Union with Christ: The New Finnish Interpretation of Luther*. Grand Rapids: Eerdmans, 1998.

Burger, Hans. *Being in Christ: A Biblical and Systematic Investigation in a Reformed Perspective*. Eugene, OR: Wipf & Stock, 2009.

Campbell, Constantine R. *Paul and Union with Christ: An Exegetical and Theological Study*. Grand Rapids: Zondervan, 2012.

Campbell, Douglas Atchison. *The Deliverance of God: An Apocalyptic Rereading of Justification in Paul*. Grand Rapids: Eerdmans, 2009.

Canlis, Julie. *Calvin's Ladder: A Spiritual Theology of Ascent and Ascension*. Grand Rapids: Eerdmans, 2010.

Chester, Stephen. *Reading Paul with the Reformers: Reconciling Old and New Perspectives*. Grand Rapids: Eerdmans, 2017.

Christensen, Michael J., and Jeffrey A. Wittung, eds. *Partakers of the Divine Nature: The History and Development of Deification in the Christian Traditions*. Grand Rapids: Baker Academic, 2008.

Collins, Paul M. *Partaking in Divine Nature: Deification and Communion*. London: T&T Clark, 2010.

Davey, Wesley Thomas. *Suffering as Participation with Christ in the Pauline Corpus*. Minneapolis: Fortress, 2019.

Deissmann, Adolf. *Paul: A Study in Social and Religious History*. Translated by William E. Wilson. London: Hodder & Stoughton, 1926.

Downs, David J., and Benjamin J. Lappenga. *The Faithfulness of the Risen Christ: Pistis and the Exalted Lord in the Pauline Letters*. Waco: Baylor University Press, 2019.

Dunn, James D. G. *The Theology of Paul the Apostle*. Grand Rapids: Eerdmans, 1998.

Eastman, Susan Grove. *Paul and the Person: Reframing Paul's Anthropology*. Grand Rapids: Eerdmans, 2017.

Evans, William B. *Imputation and Impartation: Union with Christ in American Reformed Theology*. Eugene, OR: Wipf & Stock, 2008.

Ex Auditu 33 (2017). This issue of a journal committed to theological interpretation of Scripture is devoted to participation.

Fiddes, Paul S. *Participating in God: A Pastoral Doctrine of the Trinity*. Louisville: Westminster John Knox, 2000.

Gorman, Michael. *Becoming the Gospel: Paul, Participation, and Mission*. Grand Rapids: Eerdmans, 2015.

———. *Cruciformity: Paul's Narrative Spirituality of the Cross*. Grand Rapids: Eerdmans, 2001.

———. *Inhabiting the Cruciform God: Kenosis, Justification, and Theosis in Paul's Narrative Soteriology*. Grand Rapids: Eerdmans, 2009.

———. *Participating in Christ: Explorations in Paul's Theology and Spirituality*. Grand Rapids: Baker Academic, 2019.

Gupta, Nijay K. *Paul and the Language of Faith*. Grand Rapids: Eerdmans, 2020.

Horton, Michael S. *Covenant and Salvation: Union with Christ*. Louisville: Westminster John Knox, 2007.

Letham, Robert. *Union with Christ in Scripture, History, and Theology*. Phillipsburg, NJ: P&R, 2011.

Litwa, M. David. *We Are Being Transformed: Deification in Paul's Soteriology*. Beihefte zur Zeitschrift für die neutestamentliche Wissenschaft 187. Berlin: de Gruyter, 2012.

Macaskill, Grant. *Living in Union with Christ: Paul's Gospel and Christian Moral Identity*. Grand Rapids: Baker Academic, 2019.

———. *Union with Christ in the New Testament*. Oxford: Oxford University Press, 2013.

Malatesta, Edward. *Interiority and Covenant: A Study of* εἶναι ἐν *and* μένειν ἐν *in the First Letter of Saint John*. Analecta Biblica 69. Rome: Biblical Institute Press, 1978.

Morgan, Teresa. *Roman Faith and Christian Faith: Pistis and Fides in the Early Roman Empire and Early Churches*. Oxford: Oxford University Press, 2015.

Neder, Adam. *Participation in Christ: An Entry into Karl Barth's "Church Dogmatics."* Columbia Series in Reformed Theology. Louisville: Westminster John Knox, 2009.

Pifer, Jeanette Hagen. *Faith as Participation: An Exegetical Study of Some Key Pauline Texts*. Wissenschaftliche Untersuchungen zum Neuen Testament 2/486. Tübingen: Mohr Siebeck, 2019.

Powers, Daniel G. *Salvation through Participation: An Examination of the Notion of the Believers' Corporate Unity with Christ in Early Christian Soteriology*. Leuven: Peeters, 2001.

Preiss, Théo. *Life in Christ*. Translated by Harold Knight. Studies in Biblical Theology 13. Chicago: Allenson, 1954.

Ross, Peter. *Pneumatology and Union: John Calvin and the Pentecostals*. Eugene, OR: Pickwick, 2019.

Russell, Norman. *The Doctrine of Deification in the Greek Patristic Tradition*. Oxford Early Christian Studies. Oxford: Oxford University Press, 2004.

Sanders, E. P. *Paul and Palestinian Judaism: A Comparison of Patterns of Religion*. Philadelphia: Fortress, 1977.

Schweitzer, Albert. *The Mysticism of Paul the Apostle*. Translated by William Montgomery. London: Black, 1931.

Smedes, Lewis B. *Union with Christ: A Biblical View of New Life in Jesus Christ*. Grand Rapids: Eerdmans, 1983.

Smit, Peter-Ben. *Paradigms of Being in Christ: A Study of the Epistle to the Philippians*. London: Bloomsbury, 2013.

Starr, James M. *Sharers in Divine Nature: 2 Peter 1:4 in Its Hellenistic Context*. Coniectanea Biblica: New Testament Series 33. Stockholm: Almqvist & Wiksell International, 2000.

Stewart, James S. *A Man in Christ: The Vital Elements of St. Paul's Religion*. London: Hodder & Stoughton, 1933.

Tannehill, Robert C. *Dying and Rising with Christ: A Study in Pauline Theology*. Berlin: Töpelmann, 1967. Reprint, Eugene, OR: Wipf & Stock, 2006.

Thate, Michael J., Kevin J. Vanhoozer, and Constantine R. Campbell, eds. *"In Christ" in Paul: Explorations in Paul's Theology of Union and Participation*. Wissenschaftliche Untersuchungen zum Neuen Testament 2/384. Tübingen: Mohr Siebeck, 2014.

Wikenhauser, Alfred. *Pauline Mysticism: Christ in the Mystical Teaching of St. Paul*. Translated by Joseph Cunningham. New York: Herder & Herder, 1960.

Wilbourne, Rankin. *Union with Christ: The Way to Know and Enjoy God*. Colorado Springs: David C. Cook, 2016.

Ziegler, Geordie W. *Trinitarian Grace and Participation: An Entry into the Theology of T. F. Torrance*. Minneapolis: Fortress, 2017.

INDEX OF AUTHORS

INDEX OF SCRIPTURE AND ANCIENT WRITINGS

16:24–26 116n2
16:25 146n19
16:26 121n7
18:6 95n12
18:20 88
18:22 76n3
18:23–34 174
19:28 92n4
20:28 79n9, 88
21:12–17 78
21:18–22 78
21:28–32 78
21:33–45 78
22:1–14 78
23:37–39 78
25:31–46 83
25:40 88, 123
26:26–28 88
26:26–29 62
26:28 79n9
27:37 80
28:19 137
28:20 48, 88

Mark

1:9 137nn6–7
1:27 87n21
2:19 77
2:22 87n21
4:11 87n21
6:1–6 83n13
7:24–30 78n6
8:34–36 116n2
8:34–38 89n22
8:35 77, 146n19
8:37 121n7
9:42 95n12
10:45 79n9
11:12–13 78
11:15–17 78

12:1–12 78
14:22–25 62
14:24 79n9

Luke

1:30 107n6
1:32–33 75
1:69 75
2:11 75
2:26–32 75
4:16–21 83–87
4:18–19 63
4:22 107n6
4:32 87n21
5:34 77
5:37–38 87n21
6:20 78
7:1–10 78n6
7:18–23 85
7:31–34 77
8:10 87n21
9:23–25 116n2
9:23–27 89n22
9:24 146n19
10:17–24 77n5
10:21–22 87
10:23–24 77
11:31–32 77n5
12:5 110
12:32 77n5
12:58 121n7
13:6–9 78
13:28–29 79
13:34–35 78
14:15–24 77, 78, 79
14:25–33 89n22
14:27 89n22
15:11–32 77
17:33 89n22
19:11–27 78

19:45–46 78
20:9–18 78
22:18–20 62
22:19–22 79n9

John

1:1–18 87, 91–92
1:9 97
1:13 92
1:14–18 91–92, 100
1:18 92n2
1:32–33 93, 94
1:32–39 94
1:38–39 94
1:39 94n10
1:43 89
2:14–16 78
2:22 75
2:23 95n13
3:1–8 92, 93
3:3 93
3:3–8 87n19
3:4 93n6
3:5 93
3:5–6 108n9
3:6 93, 97, 144n15, 160
3:7 93
3:8 93
3:19 167
3:21 98n18
3:31–35 92n3
4:10–14 96
4:10–15 155
4:23 81n12
4:32–34 155
4:40 94n10
4:46–54 78n6
5:17–30 92n3
5:24 99n20, 167
5:38 93
6:27–63 155

Printed in the USA
CPSIA information can be obtained
at www.ICGtesting.com
LVHW091739081123
763306LV00003B/14